T0155977

Lecture Notes of the Institute for Computer Sciences, Social Informatics and Telecommunications Engineering 489

Editorial Board Members

Ozgur Akan, *Middle East Technical University, Ankara, Türkiye*
Paolo Bellavista, *University of Bologna, Bologna, Italy*
Jiannong Cao, *Hong Kong Polytechnic University, Hong Kong, China*
Geoffrey Coulson, *Lancaster University, Lancaster, UK*
Falko Dressler, *University of Erlangen, Erlangen, Germany*
Domenico Ferrari, *Università Cattolica Piacenza, Piacenza, Italy*
Mario Gerla, *UCLA, Los Angeles, USA*
Hisashi Kobayashi, *Princeton University, Princeton, USA*
Sergio Palazzo, *University of Catania, Catania, Italy*
Sartaj Sahni, *University of Florida, Gainesville, USA*
Xuemin Shen ⓘ, *University of Waterloo, Waterloo, Canada*
Mircea Stan, *University of Virginia, Charlottesville, USA*
Xiaohua Jia, *City University of Hong Kong, Kowloon, Hong Kong*
Albert Y. Zomaya, *University of Sydney, Sydney, Australia*

The LNICST series publishes ICST's conferences, symposia and workshops.

LNICST reports state-of-the-art results in areas related to the scope of the Institute. The type of material published includes

- Proceedings (published in time for the respective event)
- Other edited monographs (such as project reports or invited volumes)

LNICST topics span the following areas:

- General Computer Science
- E-Economy
- E-Medicine
- Knowledge Management
- Multimedia
- Operations, Management and Policy
- Social Informatics
- Systems

Shui Yu · Bruce Gu · Youyang Qu ·
Xiaodong Wang

Editors

Tools for Design, Implementation and Verification of Emerging Information Technologies

17th EAI International Conference, TridentCom 2022
Melbourne, Australia, November 23–25, 2022
Proceedings

Springer

Editors
Shui Yu 🆔
University of Technology Sydney
Sydney, NSW, Australia

Bruce Gu 🆔
National Supercomputer Center
Jinan, China

Youyang Qu 🆔
CSIRO Data61
Sydney, NSW, Australia

Xiaodong Wang 🆔
Melbourne Polytechnic
Melbourne, VIC, Australia

ISSN 1867-8211 ISSN 1867-822X (electronic)
Lecture Notes of the Institute for Computer Sciences, Social Informatics
and Telecommunications Engineering
ISBN 978-3-031-33457-3 ISBN 978-3-031-33458-0 (eBook)
https://doi.org/10.1007/978-3-031-33458-0

© ICST Institute for Computer Sciences, Social Informatics and Telecommunications Engineering 2023
This work is subject to copyright. All rights are reserved by the Publisher, whether the whole or part of
the material is concerned, specifically the rights of translation, reprinting, reuse of illustrations, recitation,
broadcasting, reproduction on microfilms or in any other physical way, and transmission or information
storage and retrieval, electronic adaptation, computer software, or by similar or dissimilar methodology now
known or hereafter developed.
The use of general descriptive names, registered names, trademarks, service marks, etc. in this publication
does not imply, even in the absence of a specific statement, that such names are exempt from the relevant
protective laws and regulations and therefore free for general use.
The publisher, the authors, and the editors are safe to assume that the advice and information in this book
are believed to be true and accurate at the date of publication. Neither the publisher nor the authors or the
editors give a warranty, expressed or implied, with respect to the material contained herein or for any errors
or omissions that may have been made. The publisher remains neutral with regard to jurisdictional claims in
published maps and institutional affiliations.

This Springer imprint is published by the registered company Springer Nature Switzerland AG
The registered company address is: Gewerbestrasse 11, 6330 Cham, Switzerland

Preface

We are delighted to introduce the proceedings of the 17th edition of the European Alliance for Innovation (EAI) International Conference on Tools for Design, Implementation and Verification of Emerging Information Technologies, TRIDENTCOM 2022. This conference brought together technical experts and researchers from academia and industry worldwide to discuss emerging technologies such as blockchain, machine learning, edge computing, smart cities, network security, and computer communications.

The technical program of TRIDENTCOM 2022 consisted of eleven full papers, which were presented in two sessions. Aside from the eleven high-quality technical paper presentations, the technical program also featured a keynote speech given by Wei Ni from the Information Security and Privacy Group (ISP) of CSIRO, Australia.

Coordination with the general chair, Shui Yu, was essential for the success of the conference. We sincerely appreciate his constant support and guidance. It was also a great pleasure to work with such an excellent organizing committee team for their hard work in organizing and supporting the conference. In particular, we are grateful to the Technical Program Committee, who completed the peer-review process for technical papers and helped to put together a high-quality technical program. We are also grateful to Conference Manager Ivana Bujdakova for her support and to all the authors who submitted their papers to the TRIDENTCOM 2022 conference.

We strongly believe that TRIDENTCOM provides a good forum for all researchers, developers, and practitioners to discuss all science and technology aspects that are relevant to blockchain, machine learning, edge computing, smart cities, cybersecurity, and computer communications. We also expect that the future editions of the TRIDENTCOM conference will be as successful and stimulating, as indicated by the contributions presented in this volume.

Shui Yu
Bruce Gu
Youyang Qu
Xiaodong Wang

Organization

Steering Committee

Imrich Chlamtac   Bruno Kessler Professor, University of Trento,
     Italy
Victor C. M. Leung   The University of British Columbia, Canada

Organizing Committee

General Chair

Shui Yu   University of Technology Sydney, Australia

General Co-chairs

Bruce Gu   Shandong Computer Science Center (National
     Supercomputer Center in Jinan), China
Youyang Qu   Data61 CSIRO, Australia

TPC Chairs and Co-chairs

Yuan Miao   Victoria University, Australia
Khandakar Ahmed   Victoria University, Australia

Sponsorship and Exhibit Chair

Keshav Sood   Deakin University, Australia

Local Chair

Alex Ye   Victoria University, Australia

Workshops Chair

Lei Cui   Taiyuan University of Science and Technology,
     China

Publicity and Social Media Chair

Sudha Subramani   Victoria University, Australia

Publications Chair

Xiaodong Wang   Victoria University, Australia

Web Chair

Chenhao Xu   Deakin University, Australia

Technical Program Committee

Adam Liu	Deakin University, Australia
Aiqing Zhang	Anhui Normal University, China
Alessio Bonti	Deakin University, Australia
Ayman Ibaida	Victoria University, Australia
David Smith	Data61, CSIRO (NICTA), Australia
Eric Xu	Deakin University, Australia
Jianghua Liu	Nanjing University of Science and Technology, China
Jin Xu	Tsinghua University, China
Keshav Sood	Deakin University, Australia
Lei Cui	Taiyuan University of Science and Technology, China
Mengmeng Yang	Nanyang Technological University, Singapore
Mohammad Nosouhi	Deakin University, Australia
Nikki Wan	Deakin University, Australia
Ning Lu	NingboTech University, China
Shui Yu	University of Technology Sydney, Australia
Xiaodong Wang	Melbourne Polytechnic, Australia
Xueli Nie	Anhui Normal University, China
Xuemeng Zhai	University of Electronic Science and Technology of China, China
Yang Xiao	Xidian University, China
Yao Zhao	Deakin University, Australia

Contents

Blockchain

Machine learning

Network Security

POET: A Self-learning Framework for PROFINET Industrial Operations Behaviour

Ankush Meshram[1]([✉])[iD], Markus Karch[2][iD], Christian Haas[2], and Jürgen Beyerer[1,2][iD]

[1] KASTEL Security Research Labs, Vision and Fusion Laboratory (IES), Karlsruhe Institute of Technology, 76131 Karlsruhe, Germany
ankush.meshram@kit.edu

[2] Information Management and Production Control, Fraunhofer Institute of Optronics, System Technologies and Image Exploitation (IOSB), 76131 Karlsruhe, Germany
{markus.karch,christian.haas,juergen.beyerer}@iosb.fraunhofer.de

Abstract. Since 2010, multiple cyber incidents on industrial infrastructure, such as *Stuxnet* and *CrashOverride*, have exposed the vulnerability of Industrial Control Systems (ICS) to cyber threats. The industrial systems are commissioned for longer duration amounting to decades, often resulting in non-compliance to technological advancements in industrial cybersecurity mechanisms. The unavailability of network infrastructure information makes designing the security policies or configuring the cybersecurity countermeasures such as Network Intrusion Detection Systems (NIDS) challenging. An empirical solution is to self-learn the network infrastructure information of an industrial system from its monitored network traffic to make the network transparent for downstream analyses tasks such as anomaly detection. In this work, a *Python*-based industrial communication paradigm-aware framework, named *PROFINET* Operations Enumeration and Tracking (POET), that enumerates different industrial operations executed in a deterministic order of a *PROFINET*-based industrial system is reported. The operation-driving industrial network protocol frames are dissected for enumeration of the operations. For the requirements of capturing the transitions between industrial operations triggered by the communication events, the Finite State Machines (FSM) are modelled to enumerate the *PROFINET* operations of the device, connection and system. POET extracts the network information from network traffic to instantiate appropriate FSM models (Device, Connection or System) and track the industrial operations. It successfully detects and reports the anomalies triggered by a network attack in a miniaturized *PROFINET*-based industrial system, executed through valid network protocol exchanges and resulting in invalid *PROFINET* operation transition for the device.

Supported by topic Engineering Secure Systems of the Helmholtz Association.

© ICST Institute for Computer Sciences, Social Informatics and Telecommunications Engineering 2023
Published by Springer Nature Switzerland AG 2023. All Rights Reserved
S. Yu et al. (Eds.): TridentCom 2022, LNICST 489, pp. 3–19, 2023.
https://doi.org/10.1007/978-3-031-33458-0_1

Keywords: Network Security · Cyber-Physical System · Intrusion
Detection

1   Introduction

The incremental advancement in technology since steam-powered manufacturing
mechanization (the *first* industrial revolution) to the *third* industrial revolution
of computer-driven process automation resulted in the *fourth* industrial revolution of cyber-physical systems. Industrial production systems of the 21st Century
are designed for production cost reduction through efficient control of cyber-
physical industrial components, realized through the adaptation of Ethernet
technology in industrial networking. It blurred the separation between the *office
networks* and the *industrial networks* to allow the personnel in the corporate
office access a sensor in the production floor. The blurring of network separation
led to cybersecurity vulnerabilities to industrial production, as demonstrated
by recent cyber incidents from *Stuxnet* to *Triton* in the last decades [9]. The
Advanced Persistent Threats (APT) modified the instruction exchanges within
industrial processes, utilizing industrial protocols, to cause structural damage
to components (*Stuxnet*) or Human, Societal and Environmental (HSE) haz-
ards (*Industroyer/CrashOverride, Triton*). Continuous monitoring and analysis
of industrial communication characteristics is required to detect the initiation of
such attacks and reduce the dwell time to accelerate mitigation.

An anomaly-based Network Intrusion Detection System (NIDS) is one of the
cybersecurity countermeasures that monitors the network traffic of an industrial production and learns the characteristics from its network infrastructure
information to detect the deviations as *anomalies*. Germany's Federal Office for
Information Security (BSI) in its cybersecurity recommendations on production
networks [1] outlined anomalies in industrial networks and related categories of
feature requirements for anomaly detection systems. The general requirements
category collectively needs the anomaly detection to provide overview of all
devices communicating in the network and identify the communication links
along with the protocols used. Another requirement category emphasizes on the
ability to detect unusual or exceptional activities in an industrial network, such
as identification of new devices in the network, new protocols or changes in
protocol among individual components, etc.

1.1   Problem Statement

In the absence of network infrastructure information, such as asset inventory and
network policies, of an existing industrial system, designing the security policies
or configuring the cybersecurity countermeasures such as NIDS is challenging.
Insights into the industrial system's operation are required for efficient monitoring and timely incident, *cyber* and *physical*, response. Interpretation of industrial
system operations from its communication network characteristics contributes to
being vigilant of cyber threats aimed at industrial process disruption. An empirical solution is to self-learn the network infrastructure information (topology, assets

and communication links) and the characteristic behaviour from passive monitoring of industrial network traffic, in conjunction with an anomaly detection system to detect anomalies. The industrial network's topology, communication relations, assets and protocol data being exchanged during the industrial process operations are the network information to be extracted from the network traffic passively. The detection of the different industrial operations from start-up to process data exchange from the monitored network traffic in a systematic way for a self-learning approach is a challenge for *network transparency* (**Problem 1**).

In addition, the industrial operations executed in an order create the foundation for process data exchanges realizing the underlying intended process. Enumerating these operations through the analysis of multiple protocol communications observed in the traffic and tracking their executions helps to define the industrial system's operation behaviour. Monitoring the valid operations of devices, communication links or the industrial system would detect the adversarial actions in the context of protocol specifications of employed industrial networking technology such as *PROcess FIeld NETwork (PROFINET)* [17]. The representation and enumeration of a *PROFINET* system's operations from monitoring the multiple protocol communications in the network traffic for self-learning its *industrial operation behaviour* is another challenge (**Problem 2**).

There are multiple research works in the literature and commercial NIDS solutions that model the message exchanges of industrial network protocols based on corresponding protocol specifications, and the deviations are classified as anomalies [6]. In particular, Snort rules for *MODBUS* [10], Bro rules for *DNP3* [8] and specification-based IDS for *GOOSE* [4] check for the validity of packet fields and communication exchanges. However, the effect of protocol exchange on the industrial system is not modeled. A valid protocol exchange could have adverse effect on the industrial operations which hasn't been modeled in any of the reported works.

1.2 Proposed Solution

Different industrial networking operations of a *PROFINET*-based industrial system executed with different industrial protocols are mapped to corresponding industrial operations from the start up to the process data exchange operation. *PROFINET*'s specifications are followed to correctly map network protocols to detect networking operations and their constituent stages in a Python-based framework that passively captures the network traffic, and extracts relevant information to make the industrial network transparent for analysis. The network information made available through the developed network transparency solution are utilized to enumerate different industrial operations whenever they occur. An industrial system's operation behaviour is considered at device-level, connection-level and system-level to track operational state changes in devices, established process exchange communication links and the overall system. Graph-represented Finite State Machines (FSM) are conceptualized for each device, connection and industrial system, where nodes represent the stages of industrial operations and the edges are the transitions that are triggered by the events observed in the extracted network information from the traffic. A *Python*-based framework, named *PROFINET* Operations Enumeration and Tracking (POET), that extracts the network information from *PROFINET*-based industrial system's network traffic to instantiate appropriate FSM models (Device, Connection or System) and track the industrial operations is developed. On a miniaturized *PROFINET*-based industrial demonstrator (*Festo Demonstrator*), the POET is successfully employed to detect anomalies triggered by a network attack targeted at an industrial component, executed through valid *PROFINET Discovery and Configuration Protocol (PN-DCP)* exchanges and resulting in invalid *PROFINET* operation transition for the device.

In the next section, a brief overview of *PROFINET* technology followed with information on miniaturized *PROFINET*-based industrial system under consideration and simulated industrial attack scenario is provided. In Sect. 3, the enumeration of different networking operations executed through different network protocols in *PROFINET* systems is provided. The proposed framework to enumerate and track the *PROFINET* operations from the analysis of traffic data is summarized in Sect. 4. The Sect. 5 presents the framework's usage for anomaly detection along with brief discussion, and conclusion in Sect. 6.

2   Preliminaries

2.1   PROFINET

Proprietary fieldbus protocols were developed to satisfy the strict requirements for real-time data transmission and deterministic communication for industrial network operations such as *PROFIBUS, Modbus*, etc. *PROFINET* is the result of adapting *PROFIBUS* to real-time technology and standardized in IEC 61158 & IEC 61784. *PROFINET* has 18% market share in the industrial networks that are installed globally in 2021 as compared to 17% *EtherNet/IP* [11]. Additionally, *PROFINET* is the leader of Industrial Ethernet technology in the European market which concluded its selection as the industrial system under consideration for the presented work.

There are two real-time properties of *PROFINET* communication: (a) non-synchronized real-time communication (RT), and (b) synchronized real-time communication (IRT). Within *PROFINET*, process data and alarms are transmitted with RT communication with bus cycle times in the range of 50–100 ms. Isochronous data transfer with IRT communication is used in applications such as motion control requiring bus cycle times in range of microseconds, <1 ms. In addition, *PROFINET* defines different classes of components characterized by their functionality and participation at different stages of industrial communication - IO Controller, IO Supervisor and IO Device. An IO Controller is the component with *master* functionality that executes the automation program, typically a Programmable Logic Controller (PLC). It participates in parametrization, cyclic/acyclic data exchange and alarm processing with connected field devices. An IO Supervisor is used for the commissioning and diagnostic purposes, generally a programming device, personal computer or Human Machine Interface (HMI). An IO Device is a field device in the vicinity of process with *slave* functionality that sends process data and critical statuses (alarms & diagnostics) to connected IO Controller(s) via *PROFINET*. The transmission of data from an IO Controller/Supervisor to an IO Device is designated as *output data* whereas IO Device to IO Controller/Supervisor is *input data*. *PROFINET* utilizes the provider-consumer model of communication for I/O data exchange between controllers and devices, as well as parametrization and diagnosis information exchange between supervisors and devices.

An IO Device comprises of an Ethernet interface for communication and physical/virtual modules to handle the process data traffic. The device model of an IO Device consists of *slots*, *subslots*, *modules*, *submodules* and *channels*. The slot and subslot designates the insert slot of a module and submodules in an IO field device, respectively. The module provides the structuring, and contains at least one submodule which always holds the process data with status information. The data within the submodule is addressed using an index. Cyclic IO data in submodule are accessed through slot/subslot combinations, whereas, acyclic read/write services utilize slot, subslot and index.

2.2   System Under Consideration

The quality and characteristics of dataset employed in the development of ICS cyber threat detection methods play an important role in driving the Industrial Cybersecurity research. In the quest for finding the solutions to the aforementioned challenges, a *PROFINET*-based industrial system is used for developing and evaluating the proposed solutions. A *PROFINET*-based scaled-down industrial system with real industrial components and fully functional networking infrastructure, labeled as *Festo Demonstrator* is employed for the reported analysis. The network attacks targeted at the *Festo Demonstrator*'s underlying network and process operations are scripted, executed and resulting anomalies are passively captured from the network traffic. A systematic Python-based framework passively captures the network traffic from *PROFINET*-based system and extracts relevant information to make the industrial network transparent for downstream analyses such as anomaly detection.

Network Communication. The process scenario realized in the *Festo Demonstrator* is a simplified painting process. It is controlled through network communications between PLCs, I/O devices, actuators and process-associated sensors, and PLCs with Manufacturing Execution Systems (MES) and HMI. In Fig. 1, the network infrastructure of the *Festo Demonstrator* is shown. All the components are connected in STAR topology with the *Network Switch* at the center. The PLCs communicate to bus couplers and motors through *PROFINET* protocol, whereas PLCs to *HMI* communication is through *S7Comm* protocol. The process information is relayed to *MES* through *OPC UA* protocol from *OPC UA*-compatible PLCs. In case of non *OPC UA*-compatible *PLC-3*, an *OPC UA* gateway collects information from *PLC-3* through *S7Comm* and relays it to *MES*. *RDP* protocol is used to connect a *Tablet* to *MES* server to visualize the process execution.

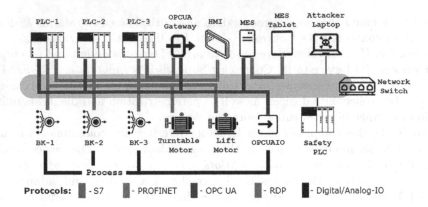

Fig. 1. The networking infrastructure of the Festo Demonstrator.

2.3   Industrial Network Attack Scenarios

An *adversary* is assumed to have gained access to the *Festo Demonstra-tor*'s network infrastructure. Within *PROFINET* networks, the components are addressed through their *logical names* for process data exchange via the unen-crypted *PROFINET* protocol. An *adversary* exploits the *PROFINET* protocol design flaw and changes the *logical name* of Turntable-Motor to *"ufo"* via the *PN-DCP* protocol as shown in Fig. 2. As a result, the other industrial compo-nents are not able to identify the component with the name *"Turntable-Motor"* and the process stops.

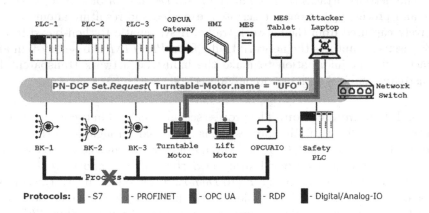

Fig. 2. The Rename Attack on the Festo Demonstrator.

3   Network Operation Enumeration for PROFINET

Configuration and commissioning of *PROFINET*-based automation systems must follow certain mode of operations in a strict order. It begins with the System Engineering operation where an automation project is configured in an engineering tool. General System Description (GSD), an *XML* file provided by every device manufacturer, contains configuration information for parametrizing the devices for real systems. In addition, each device is assigned a logical name to address it within the *PROFINET* communication. Within the System Engineering mode, an IP address is assigned to each device for communication. Transmission intervals are defined for cyclic data exchange between controller and devices. After system engineering is completed, the configuration information is downloaded to the controller. As soon as the automation system is powered on (or reset), Neighbourhood Detection, Address Resolution and System Startup are the operations followed in the same order, as shown in Fig. 3. With Address Resolution, the controller uses the system configuration information to assign the IP addresses to the devices identified through their pre-assigned logical names. System Startup operation mode is initiated by the controller to establish connection with devices and configure their I/O parameters. When the I/O parametrization ends successfully, the controller and devices step into Data Exchange mode to transmit process data, alarms and diagnostic information throughout the network.

Every mode of operation in *PROFINET*-based automation system, from configuration to commissioning, is accomplished through a complementary network operation involving specific network protocols. The networking operations and the specific network protocols exchanges driving the operations are summarized.

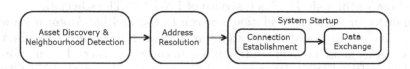

Fig. 3. Networking operations of an industrial system.

Asset Discovery and Neighbourhood Detection. After the automation system is powered on, the field device's MAC interface and its Physical Device Management (PDev) gets activated to start transmitting the parameters. PDev contains hardware-level information such as interface name, switch port data, interface and Port MAC addresses and retentively stores IP address and logical name assigned to the device. Port information is used by devices to determine their neighbours on port-by-port basis. Neighbourhood Detection is accomplished through *Link Layer Discovery Protocol (LLDP)* services. *LLDP*-capable devices communicate with their connected neighbours to cyclically exchange addressing information and consequently determine their physical location. *LLDP* frames are dissected to identify device names, number of switch ports

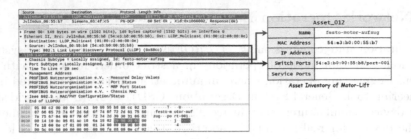

Fig. 4. The demonstration of *Lift-Motor* device's Asset Inventory filled with information from *LLDP* frame (*Wireshark* snippet).

and their MAC addresses for the Automated Asset Inventory, developed for the analysis in the reported work. Figure 4 shows an example of attributes added for the device *Lift-Motor* of the *Festo Demonstrator*.

Address Resolution. Before the *PROFINET*-based automation system starts up and field devices start communicating, an IP address needs to be assigned to all devices by the controller. An IO Device is identified through its '*NameOfStation*' information stored in its PDev and an IP address defined during System Engineering mode is assigned to it. Address Resolution networking operation for every device takes place step-by-step as follows: *(1)* Controller starts with name resolution and checks for device with configured name through '*DCP Identify*' service of *PN-DCP*, *(2)* Address Resolution begins with checking if the IP address already exists to avoid assigning same IP address twice through *ARP*, and *(3)* At the end of networking operation, the IP address is assigned to configured device through '*DCP Set*' service of *PN-DCP*. The schematic communication order for Address Resolution between *PLC-3* and *Lift-Motor* is shown in Fig. 5. The information dissected from an *Address Resolution Protocol (ARP)* *request* packet is used to add the IP address to controller assets. Information dissected from *PROFINET Discovery and Configuration Protocol (PN-DCP) Set* is used to add IP address information to configured devices. The Address Resolution networking operation performed by *PN-DCP* and *ARP* execute Address Resolution *PROFINET* operations.

Connection Establishment. System Startup operation begins with establishment of communication relationships between the controller and devices via *PROFINET Context Manager (PN-CM)* protocol communication exchanges. Through these established communications the controller transmits all the parameters for process data exchange to the internal module of devices. The process model and associated parameters for devices participating in the process are engineered & defined during System Engineering operation.

The '*connection*' between an IO Controller and an IO Device is established in an 'Application Relationship (AR)' uniquely identified by an ARUUID. Within

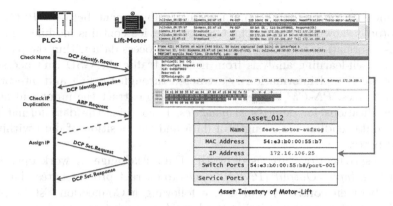

Fig. 5. The demonstration of *Lift-Motor* device's Asset Inventory from *PN-DCP* frame.

this *AR*, different 'Communication Relationship (CR)' are established for different data exchanges. An application can access data only through *CRs* established in an *AR*. *PROFINET* offers *PN-CM* protocol to handle the Connection Establishment network operation. The *PN-CM* network operation uses *UDP/IP* channel to transmit following frames in the strict order for establishing '*connection*' between controller and device:

- *Connect* frames establish *AR* and *CRs* channels.
- *Write* frames parametrize the device *submodules*.
- *DControl* frames mark the end of parametrization from the controller.
- *CControl* frames mark the validation check of parameters, data structure build up and application readiness from the device.

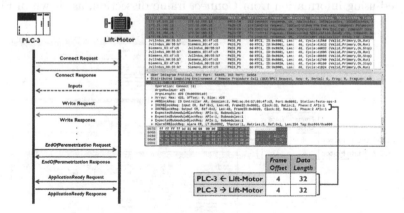

Fig. 6. The Connection Establishment handshake between *PLC-3* and *Lift-Motor*.

The first successful exchange of I/O data after *CControl* frames mark the end of *PROFINET*'s System Startup operation mode. The schematic communication order for Communication Establishment between *PLC-3* and *Lift-Motor* is shown in Fig. 6. The GSD of a device contains modules and submodules information reflecting the position of process data within the payloads. Since in a self-learning analysis from network traffic the GSD isn't accessible, the aforementioned information is extracted through reading and interpreting *Connect* frames. *PN-CM* frames are dissected to extract the input and output data specifications for device's *submodules*. It contains the data format type, order of data (endianness), length of data and the position of data within the payload bytes.

These specifications are used by the Data Exchange network operation's *PROFINET Input/Output (PNIO)* frames to extract process bytes. The '*connection*' between controller and device following a Connection Establishment network operation guides building the logical network topology of the system. These separated ISO layer connection state information between network assets is maintained throughout the automation system's runtime and deviations are reported.

Data Exchange. Once the System Startup operation establishes *AR* and data specific *CRs* between devices and controller, the connection-oriented communication channel is set for exchange of cyclic process data, acyclic diagnostic data and alarms. *PNIO* protocol defines the format and context for data exchange. Cyclic *PNIO* frames are sent unacknowledged between controller and devices. After *CControl* frames are acknowledged by the controller, the first valid exchange of I/O data with `IOPS=GOOD` ends Connection Establishment operation. Data Exchange operation begins with cyclical exchange of process data at configured/parametrized fixed intervals. *PNIO* cyclic data frame is transmitted in real-time with `Ethertype=0x8892` The process data bytes from `Data` field are extracted using information from *Connect* frame dissection, as shown in Fig. 7.

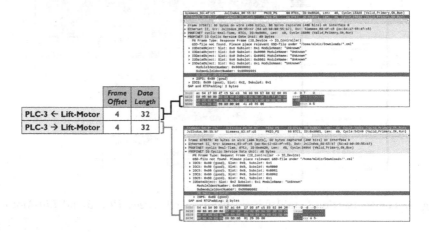

Fig. 7. The demonstration of extracting process data between *PLC-3* and *Lift-Motor* from *PNIO* frames (*Wireshark* snippet), using parameters extracted from *Connect* frame.

Enumeration of *PROFINET* operation modes is performed by passively monitoring/analysing the network traffic and identifying the associated network operation stage-by-stage. System Engineering mode is performed offline, hence, it can't be enumerated through analysing the network traffic.

4   PROFINET Operations Enumeration and Tracking

Through monitoring an industrial system's communication network, its characteristics are observed to build normal operations behaviour baseline. Deviations from the baseline behaviour could be triggered by *physical* or *cyber* threats. A systematic framework is needed to enumerate operations extracted from network traffic and track them to report deviations.

PROFINET-based automation systems follow strict order of operations. The operation mode and corresponding network operations with associated network protocols have been outlined in Sect. 3. All of those network operation's dissected information are combined to systematically iterate over the *PROFINET* operation modes as and when there occurrences are observed through network analysis. *PROFINET* devices transit through *PROFINET* operations to establish *connections* between them for cyclic and acyclic data exchange. These transitions also govern transitions in *PROFINET* connections, which constitutes the logical topology and industrial process behaviour of the *PROFINET* system.

Finite State Machines(FSM) [7] are widely used for protocol specification (e.g. *TCP/IP* [15]) [3], where the valid *transitions* and *states* of message exchanges are defined. For the requirements of capturing the transitions between industrial operations triggered by the communication events, the FSMs are modelled to enumerate the *PROFINET* operations of the device, connection and system. *PROFINET* standard, the informative handbook on *PROFINET* [13] and empirical information collected from analysing real-world *PROFINET*-based system communications are interpreted to model the operations in FSMs.

In the next subsections, each FSM is described with the overview of states and events triggering the transitions outlined in its state diagram. The transitions which are modelled based on empirical information are distinguished by dashed edges and details are presented.

4.1   FSM *PROFINET* Device

States and Transitions. FSM Device enters with *Active* state as soon as the system is powered on, shown in Fig. 8. It transits either to *Neighbourhood Detection* or *Name Resolution* state depending on the event triggered. FSM follows through the transitions as and when the triggering event is detected in network traffic.

LLDP frames are periodically transmitted by *PROFINET* device as per their `Time-To-Live` value for consistent *LLDP* information validation. Hence, *Neighbourhood Detection* state can be arrived from any other state whenever *detect_neighbours* event is triggered by *LLDP* frame. Consequently, all the

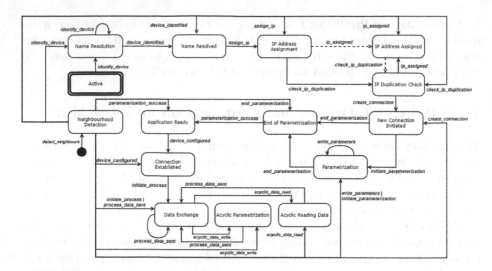

Fig. 8. *PROFINET* Device State Machine.

states are reachable with corresponding triggering events from *Neighbourhood Detection* state.

Through network traffic analysis of *PROFINET*-based systems with Siemens PLC, transitions - *IP Address Assignment* to *IP Address Assigned* and *IP Address Assigned* to *IP Duplication Check* - have been modelled. Deviating from transitions mentioned in the literature, the *PROFINET* devices checked for IP duplication with *Gratuitous ARP* after the IP address has been assigned to them. These transitions are also verified on different *PROFINET*-based systems.

Relationship Setween States and *PROFINET* Operations. *Neighbourhood Detection* state constitutes Asset Discovery & Neighbourhood Detection *PROFINET* operation. States *Name Resolution, Name Resolved, IP Address Assignment, IP Address Assigned* and *IP Duplication Check* constitute Address Resolution *PROFINET* operation. *PROFINET*'s Connection Establishment operation consists of states *New Connection Initiated, Parametrization, End Of Parametrization, Application Ready* and *Connection Established*. States *Data Exchange, Acyclic Parametrization* and *Acyclic Reading Data* reflect Data Exchange *PROFINET* operation.

4.2 FSM *PROFINET* Connection

States and Transitions. A *PROFINET* connection is established between *PROFINET* devices through *PROFINET*'s *PN-CM* protocol handshake. The cyclic and acyclic data exchange takes place through this connection. Hence, each connection is identified through MAC addresses of participating *PROFINET* devices. FSM Connection enters with *Connection Creation* state as soon as *Connect request* frame is sent by the controller, shown in Fig. 9. FSM follows through the transitions as and when the triggering event is detected in network traffic. In particular, events *output_process_data_sent* and *input_process_data_sent* are triggered by transmission of *PNIO* frames from controller to device and vice versa, respectively.

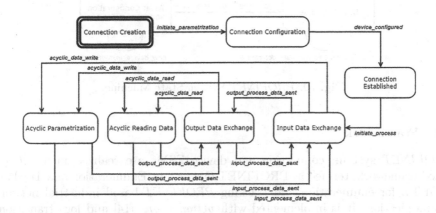

Fig. 9. *PROFINET* Connection State Machine.

Relationship Between States and *PROFINET* Operations. States *Connection Creation*, *Connection Configuration* and *Connection Established* constitute Connection Establishment *PROFINET* operation. *PROFINET*'s Data Exchange operation are reflected in states *Input Data Exchange*, *Output Data Exchange*, *Acyclic Parametrization* and *Acyclic Reading Data*.

4.3 FSM *PROFINET* System

States and Transitions. FSM System initializes with *Inactive* state and transits into *Powered On* as soon as *PROFINET* traffic triggers event *pn_traffic_detected*, show in Fig. 10. FSM follows through the transitions as and when the triggering event is detected in network traffic. Event *all_connections_established* is triggered when all the FSM *PROFINET* Connection instances have arrived in state *Connection Established*.

Relationship Between States and *PROFINET* Operations. State *Powered On* reflects either *PROFINET* operation Asset Discovery & Neighbourhood Detection or Address Resolution if the event *pn_traffic_detected* is triggered by *LLDP* or *DCP Identify request* frames, respectively. State *Asset Configuration & System Startup* reflects Connection Establishment *PROFINET* operation. *PROFINET*'s Data Exchange operation of cyclic and acyclic data transmission is reflected in state *Data Exchange*.

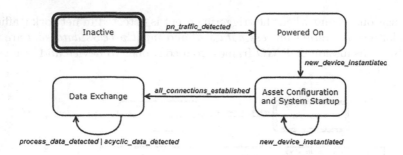

Fig. 10. *PROFINET* System State Machine.

4.4 Framework

PROFINET system, connection and device FSMs are realized in a *python*-based framework, termed as PROFINET Operations Enumeration and Tracking (POET), for enumeration and tracking *PROFINET*-based industrial network communication. It is implemented with *pytransitions* [14] and logs transitions in FSM instances of *PROFINET* System, Connection and Device continuously. Each FSM *PROFINET* System instance is identified by a name given while initialization, whereas the device name extracted from network traffic (*DCP Identify request/LLDP* frame) is used for identifying FSM *PROFINET* Device instance. FSM *PROFINET* Connection instance is identified by the connection identifier created from concatenating MAC addresses of devices.

POET clearly satisfies the BSI's general requirements category for an anomaly detection system to identify communicating devices, protocols and communication links (modeled as *PROFINET* Connection) in the industrial network.

5 Anomaly Detection with POET

Industrial networks are vulnerable to different threat behaviours, each utilizing different techniques to exploit industrial network characteristics. *MITRE ATT&CK for ICS* [16] is a knowledge base of such industrial system targeted threat behaviours, collected through cyber threat intelligence reports of known cyber incidents. Some threat behaviours (such as *Modify Parameter, Denial of Service*) are targeted at the industrial network operation to disrupt the underlying industrial process.

Pfrang et. al. [12] outlined threat scenarios targeted at real-world *PROFINET*-based systems with two different techniques to take over control of a *PROFINET* device. Within *PROFINET* networks, the devices are identified through the assigned logical name for process data exchange. The first attack of [12] demonstrated how an attacker changes the name of a device utilizing *PN-DCP* protocol and disconnecting it with other devices. A similar attack, the '*Rename Attack*' was performed on the *Festo Demonstrator* as outlined in Sect. 2.3 and POET was employed to monitor network traffic. The attack triggered events which aren't

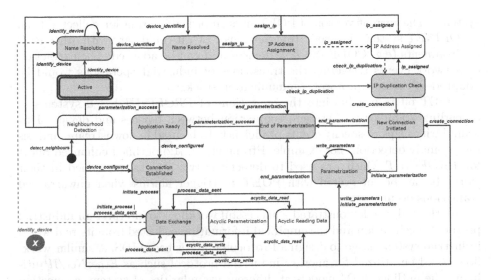

Fig. 11. The detection of Rename Attack on the *Festo Demonstrator* with the POET.

allowed for FSM Device instance of 'festo-motor-scheibe' and were reported in POET's logger, as shown in Fig. 11. The blue edges are the *valid PROFINET* operation transitions triggered by the appropriate protocol events. As per the *PN-DCP* protocol specification, the packets (x) are *valid*, however, they violate *PROFINET* device's *valid* operation transition represented as red edges, and thus detected.

The second attack of Pfrang et. al. [12] is essentially disrupting *PROFINET* network operations by establishing new connection with device. This action initiates Connection Establishment *PROFINET* operation which isn't valid transition state for FSM Device instance. Employing POET in such scenarios would also detect this attack and enhance visibility to unwarranted events in *PROFINET* networks with explanation.

POET's capability to detect the two attacks outlined in [12] satisfies the BSI's category of requirements to detect unusual or exceptional activities in an ICS network. Any other attacks that would violate the validity of an industrial operation through protocols other than *PN-DCP* and *PN-CM* would be detected by POET.

5.1 Discussion

Protocol-analysis based IDS have been proposed for industrial protocols such as *DNP3*, *Modbus/TCP*, *GOOSE*, etc. [5], where protocol specifications are utilized to build system profile and the deviations are reported. The proposed FSM-based framework, POET, can be categorized along with them as Protocol-analysis based IDS for *PROFINET*.

POET is the first-of-its-kind Protocol-analysis based IDS for *PROFINET* to incorporate empirical behaviour of *PROFINET* system collected from real-world systems. The current version of POET uses empirical information collected from *PROFINET* systems incorporating Siemens PLC, it could vary with other PLC environments (e.g. CODESYS [2]), devices and can be adapted. The extraction of network events triggering the transitions of industrial operations would be adapted to the new protocol communication stack.

POET offers insights into the operations of *PROFINET*-based systems at ascending granularity of system, connection between devices and device. This granularity helps to specify events proficiently to be used in downstream analysis for anomaly detection. For example, Pfrang et. al. [12] outlined enhanced Snort for *PROFINET* which was used to detect the two attacks mentioned in their work. It can be integrated with POET to trigger alarms when unwarranted transitions occur.

At the end, we demonstrated a successful workflow to interpret an industrial protocol specification and the empirical information collected from its real-world industrial system usage to design a Protocol-analysis based IDS. A similar workflow could be utilized for another industrial protocol such as *EtherNet/IP* utilizing the outlined FSM models at different granularities of system, connection and device. The FSM models would have to be adapted for states and triggering events.

6   Conclusion

The *PROFINET* network traffic is mapped to different *PROFINET* operations for interpreting the underlying status of industrial communication. In Sect. 3 the solution to **Problem 1** is outlined, where different protocols associated with *PROFINET* operations are mapped to *PROFINET* network operations. For every network operation, the role it plays within *PROFINET*-based automation system communication and the network protocol utilized to achieve the goal has been presented. Thus, satisfying the BSI's general requirements for network transparency.

In addition, the protocol associated communication behaviour and their detection through protocol frame analysis has been outlined. As the solution to **Problem 2**, Sect. 4 modelled operations of *PROFINET* system, connection and device as Finite State Machines (FSM) to systematically enumerate and track *PROFINET* operations. *PROFINET* Device, Connection and System FSMs are realized in a *python*-based framework named PROFINET Operations Enumeration and Tracking (POET). Its successful usage as Protocol-based IDS in detecting cyber attack on real-world *PROFINET* demonstrator has been presented in Sect. 5. This demonstrates POET as an anomaly detection solution that satisfies the BSI's requirement to identify unusual or exceptional activities in an ICS network. In conclusion, the challenge of self-learning *PROFINET*-based industrial communication networks is solved through interpretation of network traffic to *PROFINET* operations. The workflow developed to interpret an industrial protocol's specification with the empirical information from its real-world usage to develop an anomaly detection system can be replicated further to other industrial networking technology.

References

1. BSI: Monitoring and anomaly detection in production networks. Technical report, Federal Office for Information Security (BSI) (2019)
2. codesys: Codesys profinet (2017). https://www.codesys.com/products/codesys-fieldbus/industrial-ethernet/profinet.html
3. Holzmann, G.J.: Design and validation of protocols: a tutorial. Comput. Netw. ISDN Syst. **25**(9), 981–1017 (1993)
4. Hong, J., Liu, C.C., Govindarasu, M.: Detection of cyber intrusions using network-based multicast messages for substation automation. In: ISGT 2014, pp. 1–5. IEEE (2014)
5. Hu, Y., Yang, A., Li, H., Sun, Y., Sun, L.: A survey of intrusion detection on industrial control systems. Int. J. Distrib. Sensor Netw. **14**(8), 1550147718794615 (2018)
6. Kippe, J., Karch, M.: Angriffserkennungssysteme in ics netzwerken. In: Deutschland, Digital, Sicher : 30 Jahre BSI : Tagungsband zum 17. Deutschen IT-Sicherheitskongress. pp. 1–11. SecuMedia Verlag (2021). 46.23.04; LK 01
7. Kleene, S.C., et al.: Representation of events in nerve nets and finite automata. Automata studies **34**, 3–41 (1956)
8. Lin, H., Slagell, A., Di Martino, C., Kalbarczyk, Z., Iyer, R.K.: Adapting bro into scada: building a specification-based intrusion detection system for the dnp3 protocol. In: Proceedings of the Eighth Annual Cyber Security and Information Intelligence Research Workshop, pp. 1–4 (2013)
9. Makrakis, G.M., Kolias, C., Kambourakis, G., Rieger, C., Benjamin, J.: Vulnerabilities and attacks against industrial control systems and critical infrastructures. arXiv preprint arXiv:2109.03945 (2021)
10. Morris, T., Vaughn, R., Dandass, Y.: A retrofit network intrusion detection system for modbus rtu and ascii industrial control systems. In: 2012 45th Hawaii International Conference on System Sciences, pp. 2338–2345. IEEE (2012)
11. Nideborn, J.: (2021). https://www.hms-networks.com/news-and-insights/news-from-hms/2021/03/31/continued-growth-for-industrial-networks-despite-pandemic
12. Pfrang, S., Meier, D.: On the detection of replay attacks in industrial automation networks operated with profinet io. In: ICISSP, pp. 683–693 (2017)
13. Popp, M.: Industrial communication with PROFINET. Profibus Nutzerorganisation (2014)
14. Pytransitions: Pytransitions/transitions: A lightweight, object-oriented finite state machine implementation in python with many extensions. https://github.com/pytransitions/transitions
15. Stevens, W.R.: TCP/IP Illustrated, vol. I: The Protocols. Pearson Education India (1993)
16. Strom, B.E., Applebaum, A., Miller, D.P., Nickels, K.C., Pennington, A.G., Thomas, C.B.: Mitre att&ck: design and philosophy. Technical report (2018)
17. e. V. (PNO), P.N.: Profinet system description. Technical report, PROFIBUS & PROFINET International (PI) (2018)

A Robust NFT Assisted Knowledge Distillation Framework for Edge Computing

Nai Wang[✉], Atul Sajjanhar, Yong Xiang, and Longxiang Gao

School of Information Technology, Deakin University, Melbourne 3125, VIC, Australia
{wangnai,atul.sajjanhar,yong.xiang}@deakin.edu.au, Gaolx@sdas.org
https://www.deakin.edu.au

Abstract. With the development and improvement in chip manufacturing and network communication, Internet of Things (IoT) have been addressing more and more popularity around these days. Due to the fact that the end devices in an IoT system can perform higher computational tasks, there are more and more IoT applications requiring on-device local training procedures. Hence, the concept of Knowledge Distillation is introduced to solve the on-device machine learning problem–each end device will receive a distilled light-weight student model from the comprehensive central teaching model. However, several security concerns need to be resolved before KD being put into industrial environments, including data integrity and robustness over external attacks. In this paper, we propose an NFT assisted KD framework, aiming at leveraging the blockchain features on data security to solve the intrinsic robustness defects in a naive KD architecture. Our major contributions can be concluded as following 1) the first NFT assisted KD framework (KD-NFT) which initializes the chance of NFT usages in scientific fields; 2) providing a two-dimension (vertical and horizontal) security over KD data vulnerability under attacks; and 3) a fail-over scheme when external poisoning happened, to recovering KD-NFT training process back to last-best status, by using NFT history full-traceable feature and providing automatic system robustness.

Keywords: Knowledge Distillation · Federated Learning · Blockchain · NFT · Robustness · Poisoning attack

1 Introduction

As the concept of the Internet of Things (IoT) has gained popularity around these days, more and more research and system implementations have become realized with actual people's daily usages. Based on which, one of the high-level concept named Edge Computing has been brought to the front end, leveraging the features of high computational performance and extremely low network latency from modern IoT system [1,2].

© ICST Institute for Computer Sciences, Social Informatics and Telecommunications Engineering 2023
Published by Springer Nature Switzerland AG 2023. All Rights Reserved
S. Yu et al. (Eds.): TridentCom 2022, LNICST 489, pp. 20–31, 2023.
https://doi.org/10.1007/978-3-031-33458-0_2

Moreover, to perform a comprehensive machine learning task throughout an IoT system, the divide-and-conquer method has been taken into account with an edge computing framework: a large task T could be evenly divided into numbers of sub-tasks $T_1, T_2, ..., T_n, n = 1, 2, 3...$, and then assign each sub-task to an end device to perform local training process, and finally a central server collects the sub-training results from each end device, and aggregates them to a comprehensive, global training result as the output from the IoT system [3]. The most famous framework adopts this idea is called Federated Learning [4].

However, a group of defects and weak-points can be identified to the above discuss execution pattern: 1) for a typical machine learning task, a large amount of training dataset is required [5], 2) the centralized architecture makes the central server and end devices are weak to external attacks [6], and 3) the network connectivity is massive between central server and end devices, which will result in tremendous data transmitting latency and increase the chance being attacked [7, 8]. Several schemes for Federated Learning framework have been conducted, such as applying GAN framework inside a traditional federated learning framework, to reversely protect the system from attacking. However, the computational and timely consumption is excessively expensive, and not possible to directly impose to an IoT system [6].

Hence, researchers start to explore other ways to protect the Federated Learning, or similar IoT framework, and one of the choices is the Blockchain architecture [9] (Fig. 1).

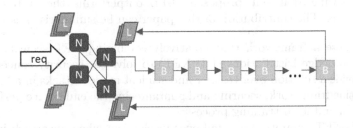

Fig. 1. Architecture of blockchain

The core mechanism for a blockchain network is the implementation of ledger—a file that locates on every blockchain network node, recording the copies of blockchain status in real-time and constantly synchronizing the value from one ledger to another node's ledger [10]. Therefore, theoretically it is impossible for an attacker to change every blockchain nodes ledgers with the same poisoning data in the same time, then by the next sync period's end, the blockchain nodes will notice the mistakes in their ledgers recording, then triggering a block reverting process to recover from the last confirmed ledger status [11].

Hence, instead of implementing a complicated and expensive adversary mechanism within an IoT system, the combination of blockchain and IoT concept will be more promising to solve the robustness problem.

To solve the problems in existing federated learning techniques in IoT system usages, in this work, we propose a new edge computing framework that using Knowledge Distillation (KD) concept in contrast to a traditional Federated Learning framework, which addressing the security features from blockchain architecture and leveraging the KD features for edge computing at the same time. Moreover, we focus on one of the blockchain implementations–Non-fungible Token (NFT), as the security method that fixing the intrinsic KD security drawbacks, majorly at the student model distribution processes.

The knowledge Distillation is a new architecture that solves the underperformance issue for edge devices in an IoT system. Typically an IoT system's end device will not have sufficient computational power, which it not possible to fully perform machine learning tasks locally. Hence, the major improvement for KD is, instead of distributing the training data to each of the end device in the IoT systems, the core point for KD is to derive student models from the centralized teacher model, where the teacher model is to be trained in a powerful centralized server with greater computational power [12,13]. However, the student models distributing process from central server to end devices are under external attacks–on receiving a maliciously modified student model, the end devices will incorrectly perform and inject malfunctions to the IoT equipment [14]. Hence, we leverage one of the blockchain implementations-NFT as the method to secure the students distribution process, which secures the student model integrity itself and provides fail-over techniques on attacks happening.

To prove our work, we conduct experiments over MNIST and CIFAR10 datasets showing that our proposed B-FL outperforms the state-of-the-art research works. The contribution of this paper can be summarised as follows:

- We propose a framework that creatively combining NFT security features with Knowledge Distillations (KD-NFT) to solve the security concerns.
- We provide a solution over teacher and student model attacks in a knowledge distillation framework, securing and guaranteeing the end device performance in central and local training processes.
- The KD-NFT supports for a fail-over mechanism when an attack happened throughout models dispatching processes, to secure the end device adopting a non-worse student model, which significantly improve the overall IoT system performing accuracy.
- The experimental results prove that our propose KD-NFT model address the robustness over both communication attacks and data poisoning attacks, when comparing to a naive KD framework.

The rest of this paper is organized as follows. Section 2 introduces the related works on recent blockchain federated learning, knowledge distillation approaches and poisoning attack threats on machine learning. The proposed framework is discussed in Sect. 3 and the experimental results are evaluated in 4. Section 5 gives the conclusion of the paper.

2   Related Works

This section provides the background of blockchained federated learning approaches and poisoning attacks on federated learning.

2.1   Blockchain and Non-Fungible Token (NFT)

The concept of Non-Fungible Token (NFT) is a high-level of blockchain application, originated from Ethereum blockchain ecosystem from 2014 [15]. By leveraging the blockchain features as its baselines, an NFT extends the usability from its counterpart–Fungible Token (FT), guaranteeing the **uniqueness** of the data an NFT secured on blockchain environment [16,17]. In theory, there are not two same NFTs across the world [18]. Programmably, the NFT complies with ERC-721 and ERC-1155 standards–ERC-1155 allows dividend (a fraction) of an NFT whereas the ERC-721 does not allows [19,20]; and FT is defined within standard ERC-20.

2.2   Blockchained Federated Learning

To protect external attacks, there are numbers of works which implement their blockchain assisted federated learning frameworks. The work [10] attach each client device to a blockchain node to achieve sufficient distribution. However, the time consumption is hard to accept. The work [21] proposed a BC-based PPFL framework with five blockchain node, each time a client producing a local training model, it will trigger the generation of a new blockchain block. The work [22] proposed a hybrid chain named PermiDAG and the work [23] proposed a blockchained federated learning conceptual framework to be used for Industry 4.0.

However, none of the above work and framework shows their robustness over data poisoning and external attacks.

2.3   Knowledge Distillation Security

Knowledge Distillation (KD) is the concept that addresses the model compressing and cost-balancing over large machine learning model to run on the small devices [24]. The goal is to use a comprehensive teacher model to generate a number of student models which are more light-weighted and retaining the most of the teacher model's features and effectiveness. However, there are a few identified security concerns that need to be considered: 1) teacher model training process can be attacked externally [25], which affects all following model distillation and student training processes [26], and 2) when the teacher model distilled in central server, there are risks that the student models are being poisoned along the channel dispatching to individual end devices [27].

2.4   Poisoning Attacks on Machine Learning

There are several identified poisoning schema to attack a machine learning framework.

The work [8] applied the constrain-and-scale technique to change the data and submit it to the server, which dramatically reduce the system overall effectiveness because of the change in global model.

The work [5] aimed to launch the poisoning attack without invading any clients in federated learning. Attackers act like the benign clients in the federated learning and deploy a GAN to reconstruct the data from the shared global model, and then flip the labels to initialize the poisoning attack.

The work [28] exploited the lack of transparency in federated learning and control a small number of attackers to perform a model poisoning attack.

The work [29] proposed a distributed backdoor attack (DBA), which decomposes a global trigger pattern into different local patterns, then embeds the local patterns into different adversarial parties.

All the works show the fact that attacks over the global model will result in more severe result than the attacks happened to end devices/ clients.

3   Framework of KD-NFT

This section presents the inter-structure of the proposed KD-NFT framework and unveils the inner connectivity regarding layers of the knowledge distillation and web3 NFT architectures.

3.1   KD-NFT Framework

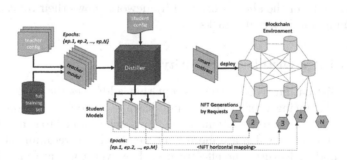

Fig. 2. The Architecture of KD-NFT

The Fig. 2 shows how the proposed framework looks like in general. There are two major parts 1) data training and knowledge distillation infrastructure located on the left part, and 2) blockchain and web3 NFT controllers are located on the right. In this paper, we do not explore much on the complication of KD architecture, because we address more to leverage blockchain architecture to secure KD's data security and robustness over data poisoning.

For the model training and distillation part, we use a basic CNN model which is compatible with model distiller. We split the teacher and student training processes into a granularity of epochs–on hitting the number of training epoch, the framework will trigger a blockchain activity, namely create a unique NFT for the current training procedure before it goes under any potential external attacks. Moreover, the framework will test on if the training processes produce non-worse training result before creating the new NFT for each of them. The basic algorithm is described in algorithm below (Fig. 3).

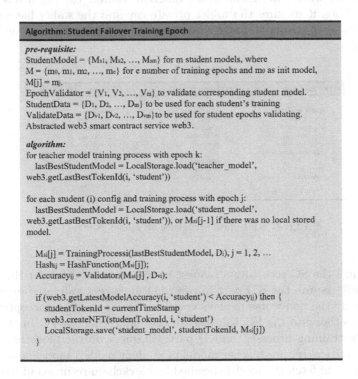

Algorithm: Student Failover Training Epoch

pre-requisite:
StudentModel = {M_{s1}, M_{s2}, ..., M_{sm}} for m student models, where
M = {m_0, m_1, m_2, ..., m_e} for e number of training epochs and m_0 as init model,
M[j] = m_j.
EpochValidator = {V_1, V_2, ..., V_m} to validate corresponding student model.
StudentData = {D_1, D_2, ..., D_m} to be used for each student's training
ValidateData = {D_{v1}, D_{v2}, ..., D_{vm}} to be used for student epochs validating.
Abstracted web3 smart contract service web3.

algorithm:
for teacher model training process with epoch k:
   lastBestStudentModel = LocalStorage.load('teacher_model',
web3.getLastBestTokenId(i, 'student'))

for each student (i) config and training process with epoch j:
   lastBestStudentModel = LocalStorage.load('student_model',
web3.getLastBestTokenId(i, 'student')), or M_{si}[j-1] if there was no local stored
model.

   M_{si}[j] = TrainingProcessi(lastBestStudentModel, D_i), j = 1, 2, ...
   $Hash_{ij}$ = HashFunction(M_{si}[j]);
   $Accuracy_{ij}$ = Validatori(M_{si}[j] , D_{vi});

   if (web3.getLatestModelAccuracy(i, 'student') < $Accuracy_{ij}$) then {
      studentTokenId = currentTimeStamp
      web3.createNFT(studentTokenId, i, 'student')
      LocalStorage.save('student_model', studentTokenId, M_{si}[j])
   }

Fig. 3. The overall algorithm with NFT generating policies

The above algorithm provides an example that when the training threshold to create a new NFT is set as 1 epoch. In the following sections, we provide more info regarding the blockchain smart contract implementation and how the system guarantees proposed robustness.

3.2 Web3 NFT Implementation

In this work, we choose the Etherum (Eth) blockchain environment as the decentralized services provider. Although the Eth network would trigger latency issue at the current settings, its property in public trust-worth and worldwide acceptance are without any argument, when comparing to other implemented private chains.

Fundamental logics are implemented in the smart contract (SC), which is written in solidity and directly deployed on public Polygon Mumbai testnet through Remix web IDE. After the success of the SC deployment, there will not be another chance to make changes into the SC, because the Mumbai testnet is one of the Etherum compatible networks and once SC deployed. The SC will be confirmed and lodged by all Etherum EVMs (virtual machines that running Etherum sync logics), where the SC state modification can only be performed through secure web3 calling and in-SC function calling. To trigger a secure SC function calling, it requires the wallet private key and the wallet has to pay for a small amount of gas fee to make sure the transaction can be confirmed by the blockchain.

NFT vertical data structure	NFT horizontal data structure	NFT aggregated data structure

{
    tokenId: uint256;
    entityId: uint256;
    timestamp: uint256;
    type: string;
    storageUrl: string;
    originatedTokenId: string;
 	
    accuracy: string;
    modelHashValue: string;
}
	{
	    tokenId: uint256;
	    entityId: uint256;
	    timestamp: uint256;
	    type: string;
	    storageUrl: string;
	
	    associatedTokenId: string;
	    accuracy: string;
	    modelHashValue: string;
	}
		{
		    tokenId: uint256;
		    entityId: uint256;
		    timestamp: uint256;
		    type: string;
		    storageUrl: string;
		    originatedTokenId: string;
		    associatedTokenId: string;
		    accuracy: string;
		    modelHashValue: string;
		    isValid: bool;
		}

Fig. 4. NFT data structure on smart contract

Each time the SC receiving a request to create a new NFT for the training epoch, it will require the KD part to provide the current validated model accuracy, and only the non-worse model's creation request would be accepted by the blockchain, otherwise the SC will discard the requesting model. In the case of starting the training process, the KD part will query on the blockchain to gain the latest entities' (either teacher model or student model) model valid id, then the KD part will fetch the model specified by blockchain returned id to continue next training epoch.

Above Fig. 4 illustrates how each NFT are structured on SC. The vertical one specifies all attributes that required by teacher training process, and the horizontal one is for students training processes. And finally we aggregate the both attributes needs together to form up the general NFT data structure on SC.

3.3   Validation on KD-NFT's Robustness

By understanding the basic framework settings and how the NFT interacting with the training architecture, in this section we are going to discuss what kind of robustness can KD-NFT provide to actual use cases.

– **Attacks to teacher training process** There are two aspects that guarantees the robustness over teacher model training process: 1) while the trainer loading the stored previous best teacher model, it would first ask blockchain the model id to specify. Hence, always the best model is loaded to continuously train on.2) when the training epoch threshold is hit, the temporary latest teacher model is going to be uploaded to the blockchain. Only the non-worse teacher model is going to be accepted and the blockchain generates the unique NFT for the current teacher model. Hence, the non-worse policy in uploading and reloading procedures prevent the under attacking teacher model to affect the blockchained model's accuracy, and teacher model trainer can always train on the best stored model by far.

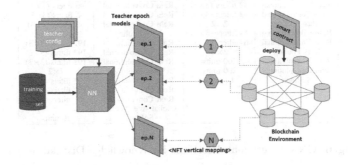

Fig. 5. The Architecture of KD-NFT

– **Attacks to student training process** The non-worse policy for teacher model training process can be totally adopted by the student training epochs. The difference would lie in the student models need to specify their unique student entity ids, to let blockchain distinguish a student model away from other student models teacher models.
– **Attacks to distilled teacher model and passing to end devices** The only pathway for an end device to receive a student model is from blockchain. By providing the entity id to calling the SC function, the student model can consequently downloaded. To activate the SC call function, wallet private key is needed, which is secured by the framework owner and strong enough from being hacked externally (Fig. 5).

Hence, the frameworks robustness is provided by the combination of the three identified aspects, which has a very low probability to be attacked and fail simultaneously.

4 Experiment Evaluation

4.1 Experiment Preparation

To evaluate the proposed framework's performance, we conduct our experiments and corresponding evaluations on two of the benchmark image recognition datasets MNIST and CIFAR10 datasets. All the experiments are running on a single machine with multiple GPU attached (12×3070 and 1×1070ti). As comparison, we perform the similar evaluation as what has been done in work [30] with the same CNN settings, shown in the Fig. 6.

MNIST Architecture		CIFAR10 Architecture	
Relu Convolutional	32 filters (3×3)	Relu Convolutional	96 filters (3×3)
Relu Convolutional	32 filters (3×3)	Relu Convolutional	96 filters (3×3)
Max Pooling	2×2	Relu Convolutional	96 filters (3×3)
Relu Convolutional	64 filters (3×3)	Max Pooling	2×2
Relu Convolutional	64 filters (3×3)	Relu Convolutional	192 filters (3×3)
Max Pooling	2×2	Relu Convolutional	192 filters (3×3)
Relu Convolutional	200 units	Relu Convolutional	192 filters (3×3)
Relu Convolutional	200 units	Max Pooling	2×2
Softmax	10 units	Relu Convolutional	192 filters (3×3)
		Relu Convolutional	192 filters (1×1)
		Relu Convolutional	192 filters (1×1)
		Global Avg. Pooling	
		Softmax	10 units

Fig. 6. CNN experimental settings for Knowledge Distillation part

4.2 Accuracy

The work [30] conducted multiple attack schema, which were model dependent and not easy to be replicated. Instead, we calculate for their averaged accuracy over they proposed individual attacking scheme for comparison.

Table 1. Comparison of Accuracy Drops

Model	MNIST	MNIST.atk	CIFAR10	CIFAR10.atk
KD-NFT	98.8	93.34	95.59	88.92
Model [30]	98.82	89.87	95.61	84.79

The experiments are both run for 500 epochs (400 teacher training epochs and 100 student training epochs) and arbitrarily impose 200 number of different attacks throughout the whole training process. Among all types of attacks, we mimic the most common two types 1) data removal and 2) data replacing in trained intermediate models. The Accuracy shown in the Table 1 are aggregated and averaged at the end devices ends. The table of accuracy shows the fact that over 500 number of all training epochs, our proposed model are resulted in better training overall accuracy than the compared model [30]. However, the table does not show that the compared model are less of performance, because in their work they identified five different types of attacks under the two types of attacks that we mimic, and in this paper only the averaged value from their running results are considered to be compared with ours. As a result, the running results show that our proposed KD-NFT can produce a non-worse than results as its competitors.

4.3 Robustness over Data Poisoning Attacks

Table 2. Comparison of Accuracy Drops in 500 training epochs

Attack number	MNIST	Diff	CIFAR10	Diff
0	98.8	–	95.59	–
10(t)	98.01	+0.08	95.07	+0.05
10(s)	98.22	+0.29	95.31	+ 0.29
10(t,s)	97.93	0	95.02	0
50(t)	97.24	+0.13	93.67	+0.16
50(s)	97.88	+ 0.77	94.12	+0.61
50(t,s)	97.11	0	93.51	0
100(t)	95.92	+0.19	91.32	+0.65
100(s)	96.69	+0.96	92.13	+1.46
100(t,s)	95.73	0	90.67	0
200(t,s)	93.34	–	88.92	–
300(t,s)	91.07	–	86.98	–

Moreover, we conduct a set of experiments with different attacking schema applied to our framework, over 500 teacher and student training epochs (400 teacher epochs and 100 student epochs). In the Table 2 first column, (t) represents for only attacking on teacher model and (s) represents for student models, (t, s) represents both teacher and student models are under attacks. From the running result, we can conclude following facts:

- The number of attacks negatively affects the framework's overall accuracy. However the results for 300 attacks out of 500 training epochs are still acceptable over different datasets–above 0.91 accuracy for MNIST dataset and nearly 0.87 for CIFAR10 dataset.
- Within the same number of attacks, teacher model's attack affect more negatively than student models attacks to the final running accuracy, which indicates the guarantees on protection and robustness over teacher model are of more importance than student models–one attack on teacher model is equal to 3-4 attacks on student models in downgrading the overall framework accuracy.

5   Conclusion

This paper proposes a robust NFT secured Knowledge Distillation framework (KD-NFT). It is the first framework that addresses the security features over Non-Fungible Token into machine learning fields, and provides a solution in recover the training procedure by leveraging the blockchain features. The experiments show the proposed framework can produce decent effectiveness over both model accuracy and robustness when attacks happened.

References

1. Sachs, J., et al.: Adaptive 5G low-latency communication for tactile internet services. Proc. IEEE **107**(2), 325–349 (2018)
2. Shalf, J.: The future of computing beyond Moore's law. Phil. Trans. Royal Soc. A **378**(2166), 20190061 (2020)
3. Chen, J., Ran, X.: Deep learning with edge computing: a review. Proc. IEEE **107**(8), 1655–1674 (2019)
4. Yang, Q., Liu, Y., Chen, T., Tong, Y.: Federated machine learning: concept and applications. ACM Trans. Intell. Syst. Technol. (TIST) **10**(2), 1–19 (2019)
5. Zhang, J., Chen, J., Wu, D., Chen, B., Yu, S.: Poisoning attack in federated learning using generative adversarial nets. In: 2019 18th IEEE International Conference on Trust, Security and Privacy in Computing and Communications/13th IEEE International Conference on Big Data Science and Engineering (TrustCom/BigDataSE), pp. 374–380. IEEE (2019)
6. Zhao, Y., Chen, J., Zhang, J., Wu, D., Blumenstein, M., Yu, S.: Detecting and mitigating poisoning attacks in federated learning using generative adversarial networks. Concurr. Comput. Pract. Exp. **34**, e5906 (2020)
7. Konečný, J., McMahan, H.B., Yu, F.X., Richtárik, P., Suresh, A.T., Bacon, D.: Federated learning: strategies for improving communication efficiency. arXiv preprint arXiv:1610.05492 (2016)
8. Bagdasaryan, E., Veit, A., Hua, Y., Estrin, D., Shmatikov, V.: How to backdoor federated learning. In: International Conference on Artificial Intelligence and Statistics, pp. 2938–2948 (2020)
9. Zheng, Z., Xie, S., Dai, H.-N., Chen, X., Wang, H.: Blockchain challenges and opportunities: a survey. Int. J. Web Grid Serv. **14**(4), 352–375 (2018)
10. Kim, H., Park, J., Bennis, M., Kim, S.-L.: Blockchained on-device federated learning. IEEE Commun. Lett. **24**(6), 1279–1283 (2019)
11. Lu, Y., Huang, X., Dai, Y., Maharjan, S., Zhang, Y.: Blockchain and federated learning for privacy-preserved data sharing in industrial IoT. IEEE Trans. Ind. Inf. **16**(6), 4177–4186 (2019)
12. Heo, B., Lee, M., Yun, S., Choi, J.Y.: Knowledge distillation with adversarial samples supporting decision boundary. In: Proceedings of the AAAI Conference on Artificial Intelligence, vol. 33, no. 01, pp. 3771–3778 (2019)
13. Shao, R., Yi, J., Chen, P.-Y., Hsieh, C.-J.: How and when adversarial robustness transfers in knowledge distillation? arXiv preprint arXiv:2110.12072 (2021)
14. Wang, H., Deng, Y., Yoo, S., Ling, H., Lin, Y.: AGKD-BML: defense against adversarial attack by attention guided knowledge distillation and bi-directional metric learning. In Proceedings of the IEEE/CVF International Conference on Computer Vision, pp. 7658–7667 (2021)

15. Wang, Q., Li, R., Wang, Q., Chen, S.: Non-fungible token (NFT): overview, evaluation, opportunities and challenges. arXiv preprint arXiv:2105.07447 (2021)
16. Chohan, U.W.: Non-fungible tokens: blockchains, scarcity, and value. In: Critical Blockchain Research Initiative (CBRI) Working Papers (2021)
17. Dowling, M.: Is non-fungible token pricing driven by cryptocurrencies? Finan. Res. Lett. **44**, 102097 (2022)
18. Ante, L.: The non-fungible token (nft) market and its relationship with bitcoin and ethereum. FinTech **1**(3), 216–224 (2022)
19. Pirker, D., Fischer, T., Witschnig, H., Steger, C.: Velink-a blockchain-based shared mobility platform for private and commercial vehicles utilizing erc-721 tokens. In: 2021 IEEE 5th International Conference on Cryptography, Security and Privacy (CSP), pp. 62–67. IEEE (2021)
20. Kim, M., Hilton, B., Burks, Z., Reyes, J.: Integrating blockchain, smart contract-tokens, and iot to design a food traceability solution. In: IEEE 9th annual information technology, electronics and mobile communication conference (IEMCON), pp. 335–340. IEEE (2018)
21. Awan, S., Li, F., Luo, B., Liu, M.: Poster: a reliable and accountable privacy-preserving federated learning framework using the blockchain. In: Proceedings of the 2019 ACM SIGSAC Conference on Computer and Communications Security, pp. 2561–2563 (2019)
22. Lu, Y., Huang, X., Zhang, K., Maharjan, S., Zhang, Y.: Blockchain empowered asynchronous federated learning for secure data sharing in internet of vehicles. IEEE Trans. Veh. Technol. **69**(4), 4298–4311 (2020)
23. Qu, Y., Pokhrel, S.R., Garg, S., Gao, L., Xiang, Y.: A blockchained federated learning framework for cognitive computing in industry 4.0 networks. IEEE Trans. Ind. Inf. (2020)
24. Gou, J., Yu, B., Maybank, S.J., Tao, D.: Knowledge distillation: a survey. Int. J. Comput. Vision **129**(6), 1789–1819 (2021)
25. Zhang, Z., Wu, T.: Learning ordered top-k adversarial attacks via adversarial distillation. In: Proceedings of the IEEE/CVF Conference on Computer Vision and Pattern Recognition Workshops, pp. 776–777 (2020)
26. Maroto, J., Ortiz-Jiménez, G., Frossard, P.: On the benefits of knowledge distillation for adversarial robustness. arXiv preprint arXiv:2203.07159 (2022)
27. Yoshida, K., Fujino, T.: Disabling backdoor and identifying poison data by using knowledge distillation in backdoor attacks on deep neural networks. In: Proceedings of the 13th ACM Workshop on Artificial Intelligence and Security, pp. 117–127 (2020)
28. Bhagoji, A.N., Chakraborty, S., Mittal, P., Calo, S.: Analyzing federated learning through an adversarial lens. In: International Conference on Machine Learning, pp. 634–643 (2019)
29. Xie, C., Huang, K., Chen, P.-Y., Li, B.: Dba: distributed backdoor attacks against federated learning. In: International Conference on Learning Representations (2019)
30. Mirzaeian, A., Kosecka, J., Homayoun, H., Mohsenin, T., Sasan, A.: Diverse knowledge distillation (dkd): a solution for improving the robustness of ensemble models against adversarial attacks. In: 22nd International Symposium on Quality Electronic Design (ISQED), PP. 319–324. IEEE (2021)

Web Bot Detection Based on Hidden Features of HTTP Access Log

Kaiyuan Li[1], Mingrong Xiang[2]($\boxtimes$), Mitalkumar Kakaiya[1], Shashank Kaul[1], and Xiaodong Wang[3]

[1] Webjet Limited, Melbourne, Australia
[2] Deakin University, Geelong, Australia
mxiang@deakin.edu.au
[3] Victoria University, Melbourne, Australia
tony.wang@vu.edu.au
https://www.webjetlimited.com, https://www.deakin.edu.au,
https://www.vu.edu.au/

Abstract. Web bot generates a large fraction of traffic on present-day Web servers. It not only introduces a threat to website security, performance and user privacy but also raises concerns about valuable information and digital asset scripting. Much research explored traffic features, tagging legitimate users and bot traffic, and created some efficient machine-learning models to detect web bots. However, previous machine learning methods used to detect web bots based on the observable raw data, that have become more challenging with the increasingly diverse and complex logic and technologies of web bots. In this research, we proposed the Autoencoder-based method to detect the web bot, distinguishing the HTTP access behaviours between humans and web bots. Our method aims to find the hidden features from the raw HTTP access data and allow for clustering the web bots with scattered raw features. Furthermore, we use the polar coordinates transformation strategy to rotate the geometry of hidden features and solve the clustering difficulties caused by the randomness of the neural network environment. We compare the web bot detection performance with the other competitors, which yielded about 30% improvements in accuracy.

Keywords: Web bot · Web bot detection · Unsupervised learning · Machine learning · Cyber security

1 Introduction

In the present era, the Internet is a core part of our everyday life, while various online activities enrich daily activities. A web bot is a software tool that carries out specific Web tasks, also called an Internet robot or artificial agent. The web bot is usually autonomous, following the structure of hyperlinks according to a specific algorithm [1,2]. Although many bots are positive and valuable (e.g. search engine

© ICST Institute for Computer Sciences, Social Informatics and Telecommunications Engineering 2023
Published by Springer Nature Switzerland AG 2023. All Rights Reserved
S. Yu et al. (Eds.): TridentCom 2022, LNICST 489, pp. 32–43, 2023.
https://doi.org/10.1007/978-3-031-33458-0_3

crawlers) [3], bad bot scripting or malicious activities against those Internet service providers to make profits and damage end-user privacy [4–6].

According to recent bot traffic reports [7], bot traffic made up 42.3% of all internet activities in 2021, up from 40.8% in 2020. Bad bot traffic accounted for almost 28% of global web traffic in 2021, nearly double that of the so-called "good bot". Those bad bots are now more advanced and evasive than ever, mimicking human behaviours in ways that make them harder to be detected and prevented [8,9].

Along with the increasing proliferation and sophistication of bad web bot, the losses suffered by web companies have driven much more research on robot traffic analysis and detection, so protection tools like CAPTCHA were invented to help detect bot in a hard way [10,11]. In recent research [12], the researchers presented a way to extract the features of the HTTP access log of an online bookstore and provided a comparison of bot detection performance among some well-known machine learning methods. Suchacka, G et al. [13] proposed a decision tree-based neural network method for effective on-the-fly Web bot detection.

However, those presented works focus on observable data features and do not consider hidden feature representations. With the development of technology, the behaviours of bad web bots are becoming more and more complex displaying different acted patterns when they hack webs. Therefore, it is necessary to find bot-related hidden features in the data and accurately distinguish them from human behaviours.

In this research, we have extracted the data from the HTTP access log of the online ticketing agent and proposed an unsupervised method for bot detection. Across all industry sectors, online ticketing agents as part of the e-commerce category ranked fifth in terms of bad bot traffic intensity and ranked No.1 in terms of complex bot traffic [14]. Our method is based on the autoencoder [15] and is used to find the hidden features of the web access activities for humans and bots and provide high-accuracy bot detection results. Our main contributions are:

- We demonstrated that directly applying such well-known unsupervised methods (e.g. K-means, C-mean, MeanShift and Agglomerative Clustering) does not work for bot detection based on extracting information from HTTP access log raw data from an online ticketing agent.
- We introduced the feature extraction and preprocessing approaches for the HTTP access log, which can also be applied to the other data resources (different web systems).
- We proposed an autoencoder-based method to extract the hidden feature of web access patterns. The bot detection performance is greatly improved when using the hidden features compared to directly doing the clustering on data.
- We proposed to use the polar coordinates strategy to solve the clustering difficulties caused by the environmental randomness of the neural network.

2   Related Work

Many successful methods have been proposed to classify the bot and human HTTP access behaviours and show satisfying performance. DeepDefense [16] used the RNN (recurrent neural network) to capture the features of the HTTP access log segments, which did the classification based on the log context information. Cabri A et al. [17] proposed a binary classification method of multivariate data streams from web servers to identify ongoing user sessions generated by bots or humans. BotGraph [18] utilized the sitemap with CNN to detect the inner behaviour of bots, showing high performance. Unfortunately, these methods require the labelled training set, which is costly and difficult to get in real applications.

Rovetta S et al. [12] proposed to use an unsupervised C-mean clustering method for the bot detection and showed a higher performance than K-means, and even better than supervised MLP and SVM. It is a promising direction that mitigates the impact of the need for labelled data in real applications. However, those presented works focus on the observable data, which has become continuously difficult to detect the more complex and intelligent web bot behaviours. The web bot has different HTTP access patterns or features [19,20] that challenge people to find similar hidden features of different web bot accesses to improve the bot detection performance.

In contrast, our method can find the hidden features of different web bots and can be easily applied with the clustering method to do the classification between web bots and humans. Our proposed method is based on the autoencoder that includes a neural network constructed decoder and encoder blocks. We used the encoder results as the hidden features of the HTTP access log and showed a higher performance compared to directly applying the clustering methods to the original dataset.

3   Problem Statement

In order to do the clustering of HTTP access activities between the human and web bot, we expect them to exhibit two distinct cluster distributions and geometries. However, web bots were generally built under different logic and technologies and presented with different feature embedding. Hence, we will face several problems as follows.

3.1   Complex and Scattered Distribution Patterns of Web Bot

The different web bots exhibit different web access behaviours with various hacking purposes. Therefore, the data we extracted from the HTTP Access logs are in various complex and scattered distributions. As shown in Fig. 1, we have visualized the raw data distribution by using UMAP [21]. The samples of human are labelled as 0, and the samples of web bot are labelled as 1. We can find those data distributions of web bots are scattered and do not have flat geometry

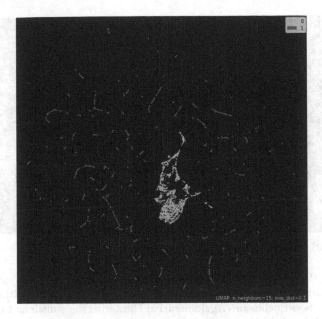

Fig. 1. Shows the raw data distribution, which are the features of inbound HTTP requests. The blue points indicate the human samples that are labelled as 0. The brown points are the web bot labelled as 1. The human distributions have a flat geometric pattern, but the web bots show the various and complex distributions (Color figure online)

characteristics. Hence, it is impossible to cluster the human and web bot directly based on distance (e,g. Euclidean distance).

Hierarchical clustering-based methods are proposed to solve the clustering problem with none Euclidean distances [22]. For example, Agglomerative Clustering performed bottom-up Hierarchical clustering strategy [23], i.e., each observation starts with its own cluster and the clusters are successively merged together. However, we found that either directly using the K-means (Euclidean-based) or the Agglomerative Clustering (none Euclidean) on the raw data of the HTTP access logs is not working.

As shown in Fig. 2, the sub-Figure 2(a) and 2(b) show the label prediction results after clustering. In the (a) and (b) the predicted label 0 indicates the samples of humans, and the predicted label 1 presents the web bot. Compared with the labelled raw data in Fig. 1, most of the web bots are predicted as human, which is incorrect. Eighter Euclidean-based (K-means) or none Euclidean (Agglomerative Clustering) cannot distinguish most of the HTTP access activities of web bots from humans. Therefore, it is important to find the hidden feature representations for all samples of web bots, which allows the feature embedding of web bots to be clustered together.

In this research, we proposed an Autoencoder-based method to find the hidden features of HTTP access data, which significantly cluster all the samples of web bots together and clearly distinguished them from humans.

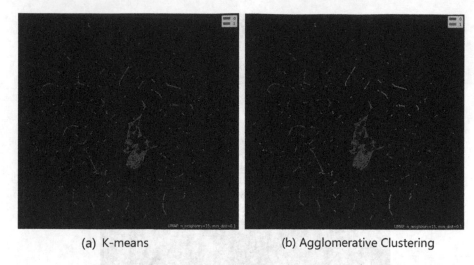

(a) K-means   (b) Agglomerative Clustering

Fig. 2. Shows the human and web bot prediction results of K-means (sub-figure (a)) and Agglomerative Clustering (sub-figure (b)). The results show that neither Euclidean (K-means) nor non-Euclidean (Agglomerative Clustering) is sufficient to classify the human and web bot based on raw data. Lots of the web bot samples are mispredicted as human.

3.2 Difficulties of Clustering on Encoder Results

Another problem is that when we map features into a low-dimensional space, the distribution of features is affected by the environmental randomness of the neural network. Hence, It will cause angular uncertainty in the geometric shapes representing web bots and humans, so distances sometimes do not discriminate effectively in low-dimensional spatial representations. As shown in Fig. 3, sub-figure (a) and (b) are hidden features embedding two experiments of our method. The red points indicate the human samples, and the blue points are the web bot samples. As the hidden features show in the sub-figure (a), we can directly use the K-means to cluster the data, but in sub-figure (b), the bottom left area of the blue points will miss predicted bot as the human (the detailed experimental results are presented in Sect. 5).

In this case, we use a simple rotation method to dominate the hidden features that can sufficiently work with K-means clustering. As presented in Sect. 4.2, we convert the low-dimensional hidden feature maps to polar coordinates, which successfully allow the K-means to cluster the web bot and human.

4 Data Extraction and Method

4.1 Data Extraction

Source data are HTTP access logs across Webjet's large numbers of web servers, in terms of a range of customers' activities including flight searches, itinerary

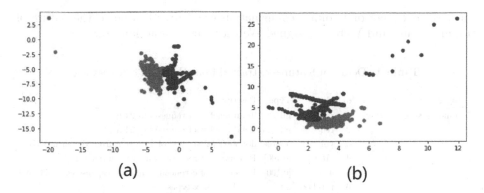

Fig. 3. The Encoder block generates two examples of hidden feature embedding. The red points indicate the human, and the blue points are web bots. In sub-figure (a), the embedding of human and web bot got the flat geometric and easy to be clustered by K-means. In sub-figure (b), the angle of geometric patterns causes clustering difficulties in a low-dimensional space. (Color figure online)

details, add to the shopping cart, payment reviews, .etc. There are quite a lot of sub-modules integrated with each main function, such as airport autocomplete functions, price calendars and so on. HTTP access logs are collected in 2022 and further processed by Sumolgic comprehensive queries to get expected statistics data. Each row represents a whole day of activities from an individual client IP, the actual IP address replaced by the encrypted unique Hash value.

In statistics data, features are extracted into two categories, listed in Table 1, the first category indicates commonly used information in many previous bot detection studies [24–26]. For example, in the Table 1, vol, is the total volume of data sent from a client, that should be within a specific range. According to the logic of the web services, normal user requests would exactly follow this logic. Also, in general bot developers would like to put some additional common information to save time to determining which information is required case by case. And the DDoS bot would be happy to carry even more data to achieve the bandwidth attack goal. Also another example in Table 1, 4xx, represents 400–499 HTTP server response code [27,28]. Well-tested Web services should very little those codes at the user request. However, sometimes it will still happen. For example, invalid inputs. Another example, Clients probably saved the URL to somewhere like browser bookmarks, but if the web admin on the server side removed that URL endpoint, the user would see a 404 response code. Seeing too many 400–499 codes from a single client can be very suspicious.

The second category is the online ticket agent e-commerce-oriented features of Webjet.com.au, which represent core functional interaction between clients and web servers. For example, most bookings of tickets and hotels start with a search page, which means we should see API calls to perform searching functions, which are noFS, noHS and noPS in Table 1. Then, users usually go through the shopping cart review page to review and adjust items. Users should not go to the payment page or booking confirmation page directly due to the nature of common sense and Webjet-designed Web services interaction flows.

Table 1. Detail of features extracted from the HTTP access log

Category	No.	Name	Type	Description
Common session features	1	req	int	Total number of requests in 24 h
	2	req	int	Total number of requests in 24 h
	3	vol	double	double Total volume of data sent from the client [KB]
	4	eRefR	[0,100]	Percentage of requests with empty referrer
	5	4xx	[0,100]	Percentage of erroneous requests response code 400–499
	6	total4xx	int	Number of 4xx types
	7	totalref	int	Number of referrers
Booking-oriented features	8	noH	int	Number of views of the website's home page
	9	noL	int	Number of login operations
	10	noFS	eRefR	Number of flight search
	11	noHS	int	Number of hotel search
	12	noPS	int	Number of package search
	13	noCR	int	Number of shopping cart page request
	14	noPY	int	Number of payment page
	15	noCF	int	Number of confirmation

4.2 Method

The Autoencoder consists of Encoder and Decoder blocks, which are the two neural networks. Given a set of unlabelled HTTP access dataset $X \in R^{m \times n}$. The Encoder block E leans a non-linear transformation, which mapping the input space X into a latent space with low-dimension.

$$z = E(x) = W_E^2 \sigma(W_E^1 x + b_E^1) + b_E^2 \tag{1}$$

Here, σ is a non-linear activation function. W and b indicate the trainable weights and bias for different layers of the neural network. The latent vector z contains the critical information of input x. As expected, the samples of x contain similar properties and should have similar latent vectors (hidden features). Therefore, we can use the Encoder block to extract similar hidden features from the scattered distribution of web bots, enabling these feature embedding of network robots to adjacent locations in a low-dimensional space.

Moreover, the Decoder block D learns the non-linear transformation from Z to X.

$$\hat{x} = D(z) = \delta(W_D^2 \sigma(W_D^1 z + b_D^1) + b_D^2) \tag{2}$$

Here, the δ is the activation function sigmoid, which returns values of hidden features into [0,1]. As we get the decoded output $\hat{x}$, we can define a loss function to approximate the $\hat{x}$ to the raw high-dimensional input space x.

$$Loss = \sum_{i=1}^{n} (x_i - \hat{x}_i)^2 \tag{3}$$

After we trained an Autoencoder model, we can directly use the final latent vectors from the Encoder block for clustering and predicting the corresponding labels. However, as we mentioned in Sect. 3.2, the rotation operation is required for solving clustering difficulties caused by the neural network randomness. The low-dimensional latent vector z is in two dimensions for each sample. The equation for transforming the latent variables to polar coordinates is as follows:

$$r = \sqrt{(z_0)^2 + (z_1)^2} \tag{4}$$

$$\theta = \frac{180 \times \mathrm{ArcTan}(\frac{z_1}{z_0})}{\pi} \tag{5}$$

r is the radius, and θ is the angular coordinate. Hence, we can have a new hidden feature representations $\hat{z} = [r, \theta]$.

5   Experimental and Evaluation

In this research, we used the HTTP access log dataset extracted from the Webjet (the detailed information please refer to Sect. 4.1). This dataset contains 8,357 samples (random selected relatively rich data from raw statistics dataset), 3,322 human access and 5,035 web bot access (bad), and the vector length of each sample is equal to 15. For all experiments, we adapted the Adam optimizer and set the learning rate equal to 1e−3. The non-linear activation function σ is ReLU. The output dimension of the Encoder block is equal to 2, which is the same as the input dimension of the Decoder block. The hidden units of the Encoder block and Decoder block are set to 5.

Baseline Methods. We did 10 trials and reported the average prediction accuracy to compare with all the competitors.

- K-means: Euclidean distance based-method [29]. It is a well-known and commonly used clustering method, which is frequently used as a baseline unsupervised method in many research.
- C-mean: The Fuzzy clustering method, which is a distance-based clustering method. It is reported to have the highest performance in recent research for web bot detection on online web store data [30].
- MeanShift: It is also distance-based data, but is designed for the uneven cluster size and non-flat geometry [31].
- Agglomerative Clustering: It is one type of Hierarchical clustering method. Agglomerative Clustering performs clustering with non-Euclidean distances and possibly connectivity constraints [23].

First, we have evaluated the polar coordinates transformation performance on our dataset. As shown in Fig. 4, there are three sub-figures. The sub-figure (a) shows the hidden features embedded with the ground truth label. The red points are human samples, and the blue points are web bot samples. We can find that most web bots' hidden representations are adjacent to each other by embedding

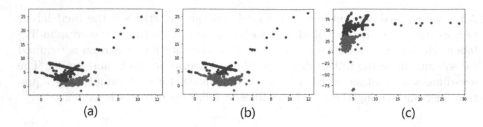

Fig. 4. An example of the hidden feature embedding with angular uncertainty is that web bots are mispredicted as humans. The sub-figure (a) shows the hidden feature embedding with the ground truth labels. The sub-figure (b) shows the embedding with the predicted labels that directly apply the K-means. The sub-figure (c) shows the K-means prediction results after performing the polar coordinates transformation, indicating that web bots are successfully distinguished from humans. (Color figure online)

the hidden features. As shown in sub-figure (b), if we directly apply K-means with the hidden features, then some of the web bot (blue) (on the bottom left) would be mispredicted as the human (red). In this case, we applied the polar coordinates transformation on the hidden features as shown in sub-figure (a), and got the new hidden feature representations for clustering. As shown in sub-figure (c), the embedding of the new hidden features were successfully clustered by the K-means.

After that, we evaluated the classification performance on the whole dataset, and compared it with different clustering methods and auto-loader with the polar coordinates method.

Table 2. Comparison of accuracy with other competitors

Method	Accuracy
K-means	0.652
C-mean	0.655
MeanShift	0.600
Agglomerative Clustering	0.650
Autoencoder	**0.900**
Autoencoder with polar coordinates	**0.995**

As shown in Table 2, web bots and human classification accuracy are similar when directly using the different clustering methods on raw data. The average accuracy of K-means is about 65.2%, while the MeanShift only has 60% accuracy. Although the MeanShift can handle problems of uneven cluster size and non-plat geometry, it had an unsatisfactory result on our dataset. We also did experiments by applying C-mean, which got the highest performance in the recent research about bot detection of a web store [12]. The accuracy of C-mean is similar to K-means, which is about 65.5% in this case. While Agglomerative Clustering aims to solve the non-Euclidean clustering problems, it can not well serve the clustering of web bots with complex distribution patterns.

In contrast, our method can handle the data with various complex distributions and significantly improve clustering. The average classification accuracy is about 90%, when directly using the hidden features from the Encoder block of the trained Autoencoder model. It yields 24.5% higher performance than c-mean and 30% higher accuracy than Meanshift. Furthermore, the polar coordinates strategy has significantly improved the average classification performance in comparison to directly using the hidden features, yielding about 9.5% higher accuracy. Therefore, our proposed method, extracting similar hidden features from the raw data with complex distribution patterns is a promising direction for web bot detection.

6 Conclusion

In this research, we proposed the Autoencoder-based web bot detection method, which is used to extract the hidden features of HTTP access data. The experiment results showed that our method can successfully generate those hidden features embedding and significantly distinguished the HTTP access behaviours of humans and web bots. In comparison, our method outperformed the well-known clustering methods, which yielded about 30% in web bot detection accuracy. Therefore, extracting the hidden features of various HTTP access features is important in web bot detection. In future work, we will continue the research on automatically solving the geometric angular uncertainty problem of hidden features when embedded in a low-dimensional space.

Acknowledgement. This research was supported by Webjet Limited, the company has provided valuable raw data to the research, those data are first-hand and were collected in the year of this research. It has made a contribution to this research and would be meaningful to the community.

References

1. Geroimenko, V.: Dictionary of XML Technologies and the Semantic Web, vol. 1. Springer, Cham (2004), https://doi.org/10.1007/978-0-85729-376-3
2. Menczer, F., Pant, G., Srinivasan, P., Ruiz, M.E.: Evaluating topic-driven web crawlers. In: Proceedings of the 24th Annual International ACM SIGIR Conference on Research and Development in Information Retrieval, pp. 241–249 (2001)
3. Shemshadi, A., Sheng, Q.Z., Qin, Y.: ThingSeek: a crawler and search engine for the internet of things. In: Proceedings of the 39th International ACM SIGIR Conference on Research and Development in Information Retrieval, pp. 1149–1152 (2016)
4. Li, X., Azad, B.A., Rahmati, A., Nikiforakis, N.: Good bot, bad bot: characterizing automated browsing activity. In: 2021 IEEE Symposium on Security and Privacy (sp), pp. 1589–1605. IEEE (2021)

5. Nagaraja, S., Shah, R.: Clicktok: click fraud detection using traffic analysis. In: Proceedings of the 12th Conference on Security and Privacy in Wireless and Mobile Networks, pp. 105–116 (2019)

6. Wang, X., Gu, B., Qu, Y., Ren, Y., Xiang, Y., Gao, L.: Reliable customized privacy-preserving in fog computing. In: ICC 2020–2020 IEEE International Conference on Communications (ICC), pp. 1–6. IEEE (2020)

7. Imperva. 2022 imperva bad bot report (2018). https://www.imperva.com/resources/reports/2022-Imperva-Bad-Bot-Report.pdf

8. Basso, A., Bergadano, F.: Anti-bot strategies based on human interactive proofs. In: Stavroulakis, P., Stamp, M. (eds.) Handbook of Information and Communication Security, pp. 273–291. Springer, Heidelberg (2010). https://doi.org/10.1007/978-3-642-04117-4_15

9. Basso, A.: Protecting web resources from massive automated access. University of Torino, Technical RT114/08 (2008)

10. von Ahn, L., Blum, M., Hopper, N.J., Langford, J.: CAPTCHA: using hard AI problems for security. In: Biham, E. (ed.) EUROCRYPT 2003. LNCS, vol. 2656, pp. 294–311. Springer, Heidelberg (2003). https://doi.org/10.1007/3-540-39200-9_18

11. Jonker, H., Krumnow, B., Vlot, G.: Fingerprint surface-based detection of web bot detectors. In: Sako, K., Schneider, S., Ryan, P.Y.A. (eds.) ESORICS 2019. LNCS, vol. 11736, pp. 586–605. Springer, Cham (2019). https://doi.org/10.1007/978-3-030-29962-0_28

12. Rovetta, S., Suchacka, G., Masulli, F.: Bot recognition in a web store: an approach based on unsupervised learning. J. Netw. Comput. Appl. **157**, 102577 (2020)

13. Suchacka, G., Cabri, A., Rovetta, S., Masulli, F.: Efficient on-the-fly web bot detection. Knowl. Based Syst. **223**, 107074 (2021)

14. Rocha, E.: 2018 bad bot report: the year bad bots went mainstream (2018). https://www.globaldots.com/resources/blog/2018-bad-bot-report-the-year-bad-bots-went-mainstream/

15. Wang, W., Huang, Y., Wang, Y., Wang, L.: Generalized autoencoder: a neural network framework for dimensionality reduction. In: Proceedings of the IEEE Conference on Computer Vision and Pattern Recognition Workshops, pp. 490–497 (2014)

16. Yuan, X., Li, C., Li, X.: DeepDefense: identifying DDoS attack via deep learning. In: 2017 IEEE International Conference on Smart Computing (SMARTCOMP), pp. 1–8. IEEE (2017)

17. Cabri, A., Suchacka, G., Rovetta, S., Masulli, F.: Online web bot detection using a sequential classification approach. In: 2018 IEEE 20th International Conference on High Performance Computing and Communications; IEEE 16th International Conference on Smart City; IEEE 4th International Conference on Data Science and Systems (HPCC/SmartCity/DSS), pp. 1536–1540. IEEE (2018)

18. Luo, Y., She, G., Cheng, P., Xiong, Y.: BotGraph: web bot detection based on sitemap. arXiv preprint arXiv:1903.08074 (2019)

19. Acarali, D., Rajarajan, M., Komninos, N., Herwono, I.: Survey of approaches and features for the identification of http-based botnet traffic. J. Netw. Comput. Appl. **76**, 1–15 (2016)

20. Chavoshi, N., Hamooni, H., Mueen, A.: Temporal patterns in bot activities. In: Proceedings of the 26th International Conference on World Wide Web Companion, pp. 1601–1606 (2017)

21. McInnes, L., Healy, J., Melville, J.: UMAP: uniform manifold approximation and projection for dimension reduction. arXiv preprint arXiv:1802.03426 (2018)

22. Danielsson, P.-E.: Euclidean distance mapping. Comput. Graph. Image Process. **14**(3), 227–248 (1980)
23. Murtagh, F., Legendre, P.: Ward's hierarchical agglomerative clustering method: which algorithms implement ward's criterion? J. Classif. **31**(3), 274–295 (2014)
24. Doran, D., Gokhale, S.S.: An integrated method for real time and offline web robot detection. Expert Syst. **33**(6), 592–606 (2016)
25. Rovetta, S., Cabri, A., Masulli, F., Suchacka, G.: Bot or not? a case study on bot recognition from web session logs. In: Esposito, A., Faundez-Zanuy, M., Morabito, F.C., Pasero, E. (eds.) WIRN 2017 2017. SIST, vol. 103, pp. 197–206. Springer, Cham (2019). https://doi.org/10.1007/978-3-319-95095-2_19
26. Zabihimayvan, M., Sadeghi, R., Rude, H.N., Doran, D.: A soft computing approach for benign and malicious web robot detection. Expert Syst. Appl. **87**, 129–140 (2017)
27. Berners-Lee, T., Fielding, R., Frystyk, H.: Hypertext transfer protocol-http/1.0. Technical report (1996)
28. KR Suneetha and Raghuraman Krishnamoorthi: Identifying user behavior by analyzing web server access log file. IJCSNS Int. J. Comput. Sci. Netw. Secur. **9**(4), 327–332 (2009)
29. Yadav, J., Sharma, M.: A review of k-mean algorithm. Int. J. Eng. Trends Technol. **4**(7), 2972–2976 (2013)
30. Chowdhary, C.L., Acharjya, D. P.: Clustering algorithm in possibilistic exponential fuzzy C-mean segmenting medical images. In: Journal of Biomimetics, Biomaterials and Biomedical Engineering, vol. 30, pp. 12–23. Trans Tech Publications Ltd (2017)
31. Derpanis, K.G.: Mean shift clustering. Lect. Notes **32**, 1–4 (2005)

A GAN-Based Real-Time Covert Energy Theft Attack Against Data-Driven Detectors

Zhinan Ding[1], Feng Wu[2], Lei Cui[1($\boxtimes$)], Xiao Hu[1], and Gang Xie[1]

[1] Taiyuan University of Science and Technology, Taiyuan 030024, China
S202115110209@stu.tyust.edu.cn, {leicui,xiegang}@tyust.edu.cn
[2] Yunnan University, Kunming 650091, China
gzwf@mail.ynu.edu.cn

Abstract. The advanced metering infrastructure (AMI) system has been rapidly established around the world, effectively improving the communication capability of the power system. Problematically, it turns out malicious users can easily commit energy theft by tampering with smart meters. Thus, many data-driven methods have been proposed to detect energy theft in AMI. However, existing detection schemes lack consideration for well-planned covert attacks, making them vulnerable. This paper proposes a real-time covert attack model based on conditional generative adversarial network (CGAN). In particular, based on the transferability of adversarial samples, we first extract the data features that the malicious detection model focuses on during the detection process. Then, we utilize these extracted features and a generator to generate adversarial perturbations that can mislead malicious detection models. Finally, to make the generated perturbations more stealthy, a discriminator is used to simulate malicious detection models to correct them. Extensive experiments demonstrate that our proposed attack method can evade most current detection methods.

Keywords: Smart grid · Energy theft detection · CGAN · Covert attack · Feature extractor · Deep learning vulnerability

1 Introduction

Nowadays, smart grids are developing rapidly due to the effective integration of AMI and control methods. However, while enjoying the convenience of smart devices, cyber security attacks also emerged, and energy theft is one of the most concerned. A recent survey indicates that as early as 2019, energy theft caused utility companies to lose more than £19 billion per year [1]. Besides, more than 80% of people paid bills to malicious electricity theft users without their knowledge. Such losses are usually irreversible and large amounts for the individual and providers. Therefore, using different disciplines and machine learning techniques to detect electricity theft is crucial.

© ICST Institute for Computer Sciences, Social Informatics and Telecommunications Engineering 2023
Published by Springer Nature Switzerland AG 2023. All Rights Reserved
S. Yu et al. (Eds.): TridentCom 2022, LNICST 489, pp. 44–56, 2023.
https://doi.org/10.1007/978-3-031-33458-0_4

Energy theft attacks have caused significant global financial and functional damage to energy utilities. It can be described an attacker tamper with the meter without the grid company's awareness, resulting in a person paying less than it should have. The large-scale application of the smart grid and the renewal process of Internet technology add significant challenges to the fragile environment of smart grid applications. As a result, utilities need frequent access to smart meters to collect fine-grained electricity usage information from users in the data center. At the same time, advanced information technology is used to conduct behavioral characteristic analyses of the collected data to identify power theft.

Researchers have designed many detection methods [2], and data-driven methods have become the main research objects due to their low cost and high detection accuracy. As an effective information extraction method, deep learning is widely used in data-driven methods because it can learn the inherent laws of data, extract features, and achieve high accuracy [3]. However, existing deep learning detection methods mainly target simple attacks, with a lack of consideration for more covert and complex attacks. Due to the fragility of deep neural network structure, the security of non-technical losses (NTL) detection systems deployed in smart grids is difficult to guarantee effectively.

In this paper, a covert attack strategy based on the conditional generative adversarial network (CGAN) is proposed. Based on existing research [4], when the model recognizes the data, it mainly recognizes the non-robust features of the power data. Therefore, we can directly improve the attack success rate and reduce the attack cost by tampering with the non-robust features. Considering the transferability of adversarial samples, we build a model to simulation the detection model and use the features extracted by the network as non-robust features. The generator generates adversarial perturbations based on the non-robust features, and uses the discriminator to correct for these perturbations, making them more undetectable and effective. Undoubtedly, our method can provide experience in developing efficient and reliable detection systems.

The main contributions of this paper are as follows.

- We proposed a covert real-time attack method based on CGAN, which misleads the anomaly detection system by adding perturbations to electricity stealing data, and the generated attack samples can evade existing mainstream detection methods.
- We utilized a feature extraction module to extract the latent features of the daily electricity consumption data as a priori for the generator, making training the generator and the discriminator easier, so that we can obtain a higher attack success rate with fewer training epochs.
- Through extensive experiments, we demonstrated that the effectiveness of our attack method in evading existing advanced detection methods.

The content of this paper is organized as below. In Sect. 2, we briefly stated related works, including attack methods and detection methods used. In Sect. 3, we introduce the attack principle and proposed framework. Section 4 presents evaluations and analysis. Finally, the conclusion and further insights are provided in Sect. 5.

2 Related Work

Topics discussed in this section include deep learning-based detection methods and security issues under adversarial attack and defense. Researchers have done many works to deal with real-world physics problems, we review the related literature and briefly summarize the techniques of the attack and detection methods related in our experiment.

2.1 Attack Methods

Although deep neural network classifier has achieved good results in classification, its potential vulnerability should not be ignored. Szegedy et al. [5] for the first time, made the DNN classification model with high accuracy get wrong classification output by adding minimal disturbance to the image. Goodfellow et al. [6] first proposed the classic attack algorithm fast gradient sign method (FGSM), whose gradient-based algorithm can quickly and effectively generate counter samples. Subsequently, many researchers demonstrated that the DNN model is highly vulnerable to malicious adversarial samples. Existing adversarial attacks can be separated into black box attacks and white box attacks, one-shot attacks and iterative attacks, targeted attacks and non-targeted attacks, particular interference and general interference, etc. based on their features and attack consequences.

2.2 Detection Methods

Traditional machine learning detection algorithms have capable to detect malicious users, which including support vector machine (SVM), logistic regression (LR), random forest algorithm (RF), one-dimensional conventional neural network, etc. However, these methods have lower detection accuracy and classification effect for electric theft. The deep learning method achieves better classification effect and accuracy, which is due to the better ability of learning the characteristics of different users from multidimensional electricity data. Zheng et al. [7] proposed a wide and deep convolutional neural network to analyze the periodicity of user's electricity consumption by using two-dimensional electricity consumption data. He et al. [8] achieved the real-time detection of FDI attacks by using deep learning. Lu et al. [9] proposed a semi-supervised deep learning model, in which an adversarial module was added to make the model have high detection accuracy and strong anti-noise capability. The accuracy of these methods can reach more than 90%.

2.3 GAN for Adversarial Attacks

GAN was initially introduced by Goodfellow and is now widely utilized in object identification, semantic segmentation, images creation, and video prediction. Generally speaking, a GAN is a two-person network of generators and discriminators. Specifically, the former aims to simulate and learn the distribution of real data as much as possible. Random noise or potential variables are then reconstructed to produce real-world examples. The discriminator is used to distinguish between raw data and generated data. Mutual competition achieve Nash equilibrium, end of training.

Based on the GAN attack, Xiao et al. [11] trained a conditional GAN, ADV-GAN, to generate various adversarial examples without accessing the target model. Mangla et al. [13] added a potential feature extraction block based on ADVGAN, which effectively reduced the number of training rounds of the model and improved the attack success rate of the attack sample. Liu et al. [12] introduced adversarial examples during the training process and proposed Rob-GAN, thereby improving the convergence speed of GAN training and the quality of generating adversarial examples. Affected by the above, the hypothesis and verification of CGAN-based effective attacks were carried out.

3   Targeted Adversarial Example Generation with CGAN

3.1   Problem Description

Let $X \subseteq R^{n \times m}$ be a set of data on the electricity consumption of customers in an area, where n indicates the number of users, where m indicates the number of power usage days. Given an instance (x_i, y_i) is the m-dimensional power consumption characteristic vector of a user, and indicates the corresponding real category label, and i indicates the user number. The electricity theft detection problem in the smart grid can be expressed as a discrete binary classification task. The model divides each electricity record x_i into abnormal or normal, and the formula is as follows

$$y_i = \begin{cases} 1, \; if \; record \; is \; abnormal; \\ 0, \; otherwise. \end{cases} \quad (1)$$

In the smart grid, theft attacks can be described as a series of malicious information bundled, expressed as $X^{per} = \{m_1, m_1, m_1, \cdots, m_t\}$, which $m_t = \{x_{t1}, x_{t2}, x_{t3}, \cdots, x_{tn}, y_t\}$, where n is the amount of information, x_{tn} is the n-th feature of the example (or an implicit feature), y_t is the label for the corresponding example. Therefore, we can regard the power theft detection as a multi-class classification problem. x_{tn} and y_t are the inputs and output of the detection model, respectively. The system diagram of the method as shown in Fig. 1. During the operation of the smart grid, since the data required for the attack is difficult to collect, even though the existing methods have high detection accuracy, their robustness and generalization still need further improvement.

3.2   Attack Principle

This paper designs a CGAN-based attack generation model, assuming that the discriminator D can learn features from the dataset X and accurately classify them to the corresponding label Y, can be defined as

$$D(x_i) = y_i, i \in n. \quad (2)$$

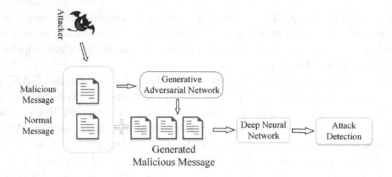

Fig. 1. Systematic overview of the method

To maximize the benefit of the feature extractor, we pre-train a binary classifier similar to the electric company's malicious detection model and use the first few layers of the classifier architecture as the feature extractor.

The rationality analysis is as follows: 1. Adversarial samples are transferable, which means that the features extracted by different models are (roughly) the same. Thus, the features we extracted with our self-trained classifier should be (roughly) the same as the features extracted by the power company's detection model. 2. Targeted processing of features that can be identified by the malicious detection model can effectively reduce the cost of data tampering. Therefore, the efficiency of the entire attack process and the attack success rate will be greatly improved.

After extracting features of the power data using the above ideas, we use generator to generate adversarial perturbations based on the features, generator G generates a perturbations through feature analysis of x_i^{per}, which can be defined by

$$x_i^{per} = G(z \mid f(x_i))$$
$$x_i^{adv} = x_i + x_i^{per}, \tag{3}$$

where z represents noise data and follows the Gaussian distribution, $f(x)$ represents a feature extractor. x_i^{per} stands for attack perturbation. x_i^{adv} is the final attack sample.

The purpose of electricity thieves is to reduce the payment of bills to gain benefits. Therefore, the resulting attack perturbation should be able to circumvent existing detection methods while also ensuring that the thief can make sufficient profits. To achieve this, we need to find a tiny perturbation to add to the raw data, reprsents as $x_i^{adv} = x_i + x_i^{per}$. Therefore, we designed the following optimization

$$Loss_D = argmin\xi(D(x_i + x_i^{per}), y')$$
$$s.t. \quad y' \neq y_i, and \quad \|\varepsilon\|_2 < \delta, \tag{4}$$

where $\xi(\cdot)$ represents crossentropy loss function of the discriminator, y' denotes normal data, y_i is the corresponds to the original label of the sample (abnormal data). If and only if $D(x_i^{adv}) = y'$, The loss reached the minimum. Where ε is the added tiny perturbations, $|| \cdot ||_2$ is a norm constraint on perturbation, δ is the maximum perturbation value specified.

3.3   The Proposed CGAN-based Architecture

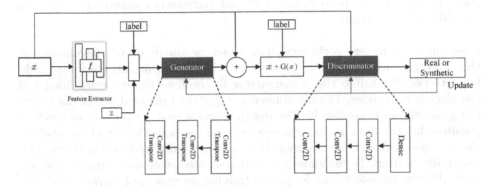

Fig. 2. Structure diagram of attack model based on CGAN

As shown in Fig. 2, the structure of the proposed model contains a feature extractor f, a generator G and a discriminator D. The feature extractor f extracts the latent features $f(x)$ (the main features recognized by the malicious detection system) from the power data x. Then, concatenate $f(x)$ with the noise vector as the input of the generator G to generate a perturbation x_i^{per} corresponding to x. Finally, $x + G(x)$ is sent to D, and the output result represents the probability of normal samples. In our method, the feature extractor, generator, and discriminator are trained end-to-end.

Feature Extractor: A recent research shown that the cause of adversarial examples is the non-robust feature learned from the training set by models [16]. Particularly, research shows that the knowledge learned by machine learning models during training is the correspondence between non-robust features and data labels. Motivated by the demonstration, we perform saliency feature extraction on the electricity consumption data in advance, in this way, the extracted prior knowledge can be used to generate adversarial examples to have better performance, Moreover, due to the preprocessing of the feature extractor, subsequent network structures can only focus on their own tasks (such as generating perturbations and identifying data), so that significantly improve the model convergence speed. We use convolutional layers to extract the features of the power data, and combine the extracted features with Gaussian noise z_{noise} as the input of the generator.

Generator: The attacker's goal is to disguise the tampered power data as untampered, which is similar to adversarial attacks. Therefore, after using the feature extractor to extract the features of the target power data, we need to generate the corresponding adversarial perturbation based on the feature, and add the perturbation to the raw data. In addition, the features obtained by the feature extractor have different dimensions from the original data, thus another function of the generator is to unify the dimension of the generated perturbation and raw data. The generator is implemented with an autoencoder, during the training phase, we take root mean square error as the loss function. The optimization goal of the generator is to make its output (adversarial example) as close as possible to x (raw data).

Discriminator: In real-world scenarios, attackers usually do not have access to the detection model of electric companies, thus they can only perform black-box attacks. We utilise the discriminator to simulate the detection model of the electric companies. The discriminator takes the tampered power data from the generator and classifies it. The discriminator's goal is to detect as much as possible that the data has been tampered, and transmit the detection result to the generator through back-propagation. The generator updates itself based on the feedback from the discriminator and generates tampered samples that are more difficult to detect, and loops the training process until convergence. The discriminator is a three-layer neural network. At this point, the discriminator has two tasks, one is to distinguish the true and false samples (the original task in GAN), another is to classify the tampered data.

In brief, the task of the generator is to generate minimal perturbations while maximally misleading the discriminator classification. The discriminator is continuously trained to identify whether the input is a malicious sample or a normal sample. The two are constantly competing, and the process can be defined as a V function as

$$\min_{G} \max_{D} V(D, G) = E_{x \sim p_{data}(x|y)}[log D(x)] +$$
$$E_{x \sim p_z(x)}[1 - log(D(x + G(x)|y))]. \tag{5}$$

During the optimization process, the data distribution generated by the generator G will gradually coincide with the original data distribution, which increases the difficulty of detecting tampered samples. The discriminator D is used to ensure that the data generated by G is similar to benign data. We define $p_g(x)$ as the generative distribution of G, then the maximum value of D to be solved by the V function can be expressed as $D(x) = p_{data}(x)/(p_{data}(x) + p_g(x))$. After reaching the Nash equilibrium point, the training will stop. At this time, $p_{data}(x) = p_g(x)$, that is, $D(x) = 0.5$. Since the discriminator simulates a malicious detector, $D(x) = 0.5$ means that the detection by the malicious detection system is equivalent to random guessing.

4   Evaluation and Analysis

In this section, we will present the experimental results. In Sect. 4.1, we describe the experimental data and its preprocessing procedure. Section 4.2 introduces the performance indicators. We then show the performance of our proposed covert attack on various advanced detection models in Sect. 4.3. Finally, we evaluate the attack model presented in Sect. 4.4.

4.1   Experimental Data and Preprocessing

We conduct experiments using a real dataset released by State Grid, which records the daily electricity consumption of 42,372 users for 1,035 days. In addition, State Grid classified each user in the dataset, including 38,757 normal users and 3,615 electricity stealing users. In this experiment, 3000 users marked as electricity stealers and 17000 users marked as normal were randomly selected to form the original dataset. Then, select 2000 normal users and use the proposed attack model to generate attack samples, and then extract 1000 electricity stealing users and 17000 normal users and the generated attack samples to form an attack data set. Finally, the original dataset and the attack dataset are divided into 80% training set and 20% testing set, respectively.

There are a large number of missing values in the dataset, which we filled in using the interpolation method shown below. The outliers are then processed using the three-sigma criterion, and finally the data is normalized using MAX-MIN.

$$x'_{i,t} = \frac{x_{i,t} - x_{min}}{x_{max} - x_{min}}, \tag{6}$$

where $x_{i,t}$ and $x'_{i,t}$ are the power consumption of i-th user in the t-th day and the normalized power consumption. x_{max} and x_{min} represent the maximum and minimum values in the power consumption sequence.

4.2   Performance Indicators

In this experiment, we used AUC, MAP and Recall as evaluation metrics to evaluate the effectiveness of the generated attack samples. AUC is defined as the area under the ROC curve, which is usually used as an evaluation index for binary detection models. Its abscissa is false positive rate (FPR), and its ordinate is true positive rate (TRP). Usually, the value of AUC is in the range of [0.5–1], and the closer it is to 1, the better the classification effect. Its calculation formula is as follows

$$AUC = \frac{\Sigma_{i \in positive} Rank_i - \frac{M(M+1)}{2}}{M \times N}, \tag{7}$$

where $Rank_i$ is the rank of sample i, M is the number of normal users, and N is the number of abnormal users.

MAP is also used in this paper to measure the accuracy of the hybrid detection model. The specific calculation formula is as follows

$$MAP@N = \frac{\sum_{i=1}^{s} \frac{Y_{k_i}}{k_i}}{s}, \tag{8}$$

where s represents the number of true positive samples in the first N scores after sorting the rank from high to low, k_i represents the position of the ith true positive sample, and Y_{k_i} represents the number of true positive samples before k_i.

In addition, we used the Recall to evaluate the detection rate of positive samples, the formula is as follows

$$Recall = \frac{TP}{TP + FN}, \tag{9}$$

where TP is the amount of accurate predictions made for positive samples, and FN is the amount of forecasts for positive samples that were wrong.

4.3 Attack Performance Verification and Analysis

To verify our attack performance of the generated samples, five advanced detection models are evaluated in this chapter on the original and attack datasets, including support vector machine (SVM), logistic regression (LR), random forest (RF), convolutional neural networks (CNN) and Wide&Deep CNNs. As shown in Table 1, both CNN and wide&deep models have shown good performance in detecting traditional electricity stealing behavior, which is mainly due to the fact that deep neural networks can learn hidden features of abnormal samples and normal samples. Compared with SVM, LR and RF, it can better capture local correlation and achieve good results.

Table 1. Detection results of the original data set

Typle	AUC	MAP@50	Recall
SVM	0.65	0.75	0.70
LR	0.59	0.35	0.59
RF	0.67	0.43	0.61
CNN	0.73	0.87	0.67
Wide&Deep	0.81	0.89	0.71

The Table 2 depicts the advanced models' detection results for the attack data set produced in this chapter. Among them, all performance indicators have dropped significantly, especially MAP and Recall have dropped significantly, mainly because these models cannot identify attack samples in the data set. In addition, there are still certain AUC and MAP values because the attack dataset also contains 1000 traditional electricity stealing samples and normal samples, which will be correctly classified by advanced detection methods. To sum up, the attack samples generated in this chapter can effectively evade the identification of existing detection algorithms.

Table 2. Detection results of the attack data set

Typle	AUC	MAP@50	Recall
SVM	0.55	0.40	0.50
LR	0.50	0.17	0.15
RF	0.45	0.08	0.15
CNN	0.58	0.33	0.46
Wide&Deep	0.64	0.51	0.64

In the experiment, we also considered the impact of the continuous electricity stealing days on the attack effect under this attack method. Specifically, the attack days of 2,000 attacking users ranged from 10 days to 100 days, with a step size of 10. As depicted in Fig. 3, as attack days rise, the AUC and MAP values basically change around 0.1, and the fluctuation range is small, so the effectiveness of the generated attack samples in long-term electricity stealing can be verified.

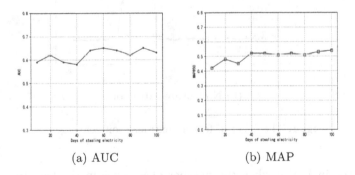

(a) AUC   (b) MAP

Fig. 3. Comparison of different number of attack days

4.4 Generative Network Model Performance Analysis

In this section, we investigate the impact of several parameters on the functionality of the generative model, including: whether to use a feature extractor, the number of neurons in the feature extractor, and the number of network layers in the generator.

The feature extractor is located in front of the generator, and the extraction of electricity data features by main users is used as a priori information for the generator to generate disturbances. As shown in Fig. 4, the generative network model's convergence speed and training time may both be significantly accelerated by the feature extractor.

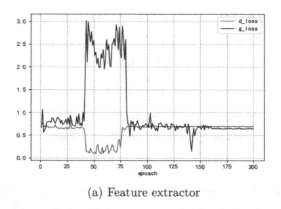

(a) Feature extractor

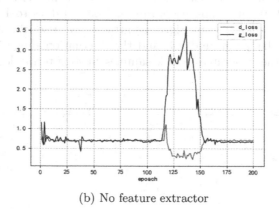

(b) No feature extractor

Fig. 4. The effect of feature extractor on convergence

As shown in Fig. 5, when the number of neurons in the feature extractor's fully connected layer reaches 300, the AUC and MAP@50 values of the detection model are both low, and the attack samples generated by the generative network model are closest to the real data.

Finally, as shown in Fig. 6, when the number of generator network layers in the generative model is 3, the generated attack samples have a strong ability to evade detection, and the attack performance is better. When there are more than 3 layers, all indicators show a smooth trend, and it is difficult to achieve better results if more computing power is added to the number of layers.

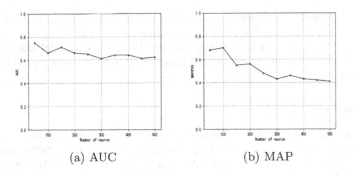

(a) AUC   (b) MAP

Fig. 5. Impact of layer number

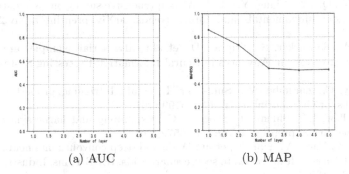

(a) AUC   (b) MAP

Fig. 6. Comparison of different number of neurons in the fully connected layer of the feature extractor

5   Summary

In this paper, we evaluate the vulnerability of models for detecting energy theft based on deep learning, when appropriate perturbations are added to the data will mislead a trained high-accuracy classifier. Based on this finding, we designed a CGAN-based generative model. Different from the traditional CGAN model, we add a feature extractor to extract the user's electricity consumption feature information. Comprehensive experiments have shown that the generation model designed in this chapter can generate attack samples efficiently, and has shown good attack performance in the face of the current advanced electricity stealing detection models. We will take improving the robustness of deep learning models as the focus of future work, specifically to optimize the network structure and training strategies, to ensure that on the basis of effective training, we will further improve the defense accuracy on the data set.

Acknowledgment. This work was supported by the Scientific and Technologial Innovation Programs of Higher Education Institutions in Shanxi, China (No. 2020L0338) and the Shanxi Key Research and Development Program (No. 202102020101002 and 202102020101005) and the Fundamental Research Funds for the Central Universities (No. 2042022kf0021).

References

1. Yao, D., Wen, M., Liang, X., et al.: Energy theft detection with energy privacy preservation in the smart grid. IEEE Internet Things J. **6**(5), 7659–7669 (2019)
2. Cui, L., Guo, L., Gao, L., et al.: A covert electricity-theft cyber-attack against machine learning-based detection models. IEEE Trans. Ind. Inform. **18**(11), 7824–7833 (2021)
3. Zhao, Y., Qu, Y., Xiang, Y., et al.: A comprehensive survey on edge data integrity verification: fundamentals and future trends. arXiv preprint arXiv:2210.10978 (2022)
4. Ilyas, A., Santurkar, S., Tsipras, D., et al.: Adversarial examples are not bugs, they are features. In: Advances in Neural Information Processing Systems, vol. 32 (2019)
5. Szegedy, C., Zaremba, W., Sutskever, I., et al.: Intriguing properties of neural networks. arXiv preprint arXiv:1312.6199 (2013)
6. Goodfellow, I.J., Shlens, J., Szegedy, C.: Explaining and harnessing adversarial examples. arXiv preprint arXiv:1412.6572 (2014)
7. Zheng, Z., Yang, Y., Niu, X., et al.: Wide and deep convolutional neural networks for electricity-theft detection to secure smart grids. IEEE Trans. Industr. Inf. **14**(4), 1606–1615 (2017)
8. He, Y., Mendis, G.J., Wei, J.: Real-time detection of false data injection attacks in smart grid: A deep learning-based intelligent mechanism. IEEE Trans. Smart Grid **8**(5), 2505–2516 (2017)
9. Lu, X., Zhou, Y., Wang, Z., et al.: Knowledge embedded semi-supervised deep learning for detecting non-technical losses in the smart grid. Energies **12**(18), 3452 (2019)
10. Goodfellow, I., Pouget-Abadie, J., Mirza, M., et al.: Generative adversarial nets. In: Advances in Neural Information Processing Systems, vol. 27 (2014)
11. Mirza, M., Osindero, S.: Conditional generative adversarial nets. arXiv preprint arXiv:1411.1784 (2014)
12. Liu, X., Hsieh, C.J.: Rob-GAN: generator, discriminator, and adversarial attacker. In: Proceedings of the IEEE/CVF Conference on Computer Vision and Pattern Recognition, pp. 11234–11243 (2019)
13. Jandial, S., Mangla, P., Varshney, S., et al.: AdvGAN++: harnessing latent layers for adversary generation. In: Proceedings of the IEEE/CVF International Conference on Computer Vision Workshops (2019)
14. Ying, H., Ouyang, X., Miao, S., et al.: Power message generation in smart grid via generative adversarial network. In: 2019 IEEE 3rd Information Technology, Networking, Electronic and Automation Control Conference (ITNEC), pp. 790–793. IEEE (2019)
15. Bai, T., Zhao, J., Zhu, J., et al.: Toward efficiently evaluating the robustness of deep neural networks in IoT systems: a GAN-based method. IEEE Internet Things J. **9**(3), 1875–1884 (2021)
16. Chen, R., Chen, J., Zheng, H., et al.: Salient feature extractor for adversarial defense on deep neural networks. Inf. Sci. **600**, 118–143 (2022)

Network Communication

Implementation of an All-Digital DRC for 100BASE-FX

Gang Luo[1], Qiangang Wang[1], Yujia Liu[2], Yuping Zhang[3(✉)], Hanyue Sun[1], and Qicheng Zhou[4]

[1] CYG SUNRI CO., LTD., Shenzhen, China
wangqg@cyg.com
[2] University of Electronic Science and Technology of China, Chendu, China
[3] Chengdu Technological University, Chendu, China
zhangyuping@cdtu.edu.cn
[4] Chengdu University of Information Technology, Chendu, China

Abstract. This paper proposes a blind oversampling data recovery algorithm LUT-DRC (Data Recovery Algorithm Based on Look-Up Table) for 100Base-FX. The LUT-DRC can recover all data in an Ethernet packet of any length, even a clock jitter of $8\,ns \pm 0.03125\,ns$ at the transmitter. The LUT-DRC core consists of only 470 LUT6, 1 block RAM, and 1 PLL (Phase-Locked Loop, PLL) and has an estimated power consumption of 10 mW at 125 Mbps. LUT-DRC was implemented on a PANGO PGL25 FPGA device and tested using a NuStreams-700 network tester. No CRC (Cyclic Redundancy Check, CRC) errors were found during data transfer testing using $2.5 * 10^8$ Ethernet packets. The characteristics of LUT-DRC and its performance make it suitable for any FPGA to implement 100BASE-FX communication without a 100BASE-FX PHY (Physical Layer Transceiver, PHY) chip.

Keywords: DRC · Oversampling · Jitter tolerance · FPGA

1 Introduction

The 100BASE-FX communication systems are generally implemented based on PHY chips [15]. However, in a communication system with an FPGA device, it is an effective method to reduce system power consumption and improve system stability by integrating the PHY into the FPGA. The 100Base-FX Ethernet adopts FDDI (Fiber Distributed Data Interface, FDDI) physical layer standard. The signal transmitted on the physical layer is the 4B5B asynchronous serial signal encoded by NRZI (Non return to zero, inverted, NRZI) [1]. Therefore, the key point to implementing a 100BASE-FX PHY transceiver inside an FPGA is the all-digital CDR (Clock and Data Recovery, CDR) circuit. FPGA device vendors only deliver the hardware IP on high-end products for the 100BASE-FX communication solutions based on SerDes (Serializer/Deserializer, SerDes). For

© ICST Institute for Computer Sciences, Social Informatics and Telecommunications Engineering 2023
Published by Springer Nature Switzerland AG 2023. All Rights Reserved
S. Yu et al. (Eds.): TridentCom 2022, LNICST 489, pp. 59–69, 2023.
https://doi.org/10.1007/978-3-031-33458-0_5

example, Xilinx Artix7, Spartan series and Intel Arria10, Stratix10 series [5,7,9]. However, It is challenging to implement the all-digital CDR circuit on FPGA without SerDes.

In recent years, there has been an increasing amount of literature on BO-CDR (Blind Oversampling Clock and Data Recovery, BO-CDR). For example, Seoul National University [10], The University of Tokyo [4] and University of Minnesota [8]. Previous research has established that BO-CDR is the main methods of implementing digital CDR [12]. It is based on the direct sampling method or phase discriminative coding method [10]. For example, The all-digital BO-CDR designed by The University of Tokyo in 2009 uses phase discrimination coding logic, the designed circuit is placed on the Altera Stratix GX FPGA evaluation board for verification, and its jitter tolerance is 0.9 unit interval (Unit Interval, UI).

The discrimination coding method uses a clock with a frequency M times the data rate to sample the data. Then select the sample value with the encoding value equal to $1/2M$ as the correct sample data [6,17]. This method has several advantages. Firstly, oversampling and data recovery can be implemented in a digital circuit, which makes it easy to implement in different digital systems. Secondly, BO-CDR can be locked to serial data immediately during an oversampling cycle, which makes instantaneous phase acquisition possible [8]. Thirdly, BO-CDR is realized in digital circuit, which eliminates the influence of noise signal. But BO-CDR has some disadvantages. BO-CDR needs a high-frequency encoding clock. When the data rate is n Mbps, the encoding clock is required to be $m*n$ MHz (m is the oversampling rate), which is a great challenge for FPGAs [13]. Because the timing closure is too difficult with the frequency increase in FPGA [2]. Secondly, since BO-CDR only recovers $1bit$ of sample value per cycle, this algorithm can perform well when the reference clock and data source frequencies are the same. But its resistance to clock jitter is very weak, there is a high BER (Bit Error Ratio, BER) when clocks or data drift away from each other. Third, it is complicated to implement the direct sampling method using digital circuits.

Defosez, Marc et al. Used PLL to generate the same frequency multiphase clock, then use both rising and falling edges to sample data [6]. This method reduces the clock frequency from $m*n$ MHz to n MHz or $1/2*n$ MHz. Gao Ning et al. Added a filter structure between the oversampling and the data recovery unit, to reduce the BER [13]. However, there is no good method to improve the clock jitter resistance while reducing the logic complexity.

In this paper, a LUT-DRC algorithm based on look-up table is proposed to solve above problems, which makes it possible to implement a 100Base-FX in FPGAs. And the DRC-Table obeys the basic principles and data laws of BO-CDR. Extensive test experiments have shown that the data recovery unit implemented by this method meets the performance requirements of 100BASE-FX.

2   LUT-DRC

The primary approach of the LUT-DRC is to analyze all possible data oversampling values and edge cases based on the data characteristics during transmission. These characteristics include features of FDDI in 100BASE-FX, oversampling factors, and NRZI code features. We specify the location of the data to be recovered in each case to form a DRC Table. The recovered data will be stored in a FIFO (First In, First Out, FIFO) to achieve continuous asynchronous serial data recovery. After being processed by the rate balancing module, the data will output smoothly at the original transmission rate.

This method has a simple logical structure and implementation. The rate balancing unit after the LUT-DRC turns the data stream from non-uniform into uniform, solving the problem of data bit lossing due to the clock and data rate imbalance. Our algorithm provides a new idea to implement 125 Mbps asynchronous serial data recovery in FPGAs, thus making it possible to implement 100BASE-FX PHY transceivers inside FPGAs.

2.1   Overall Structure

The overall structure of LUT-DRC is shown in Fig. 1. The input of the LUT-DRC is 125 Mbps differential serial data, and the output is a set of source synchronization signals containing clock and data. The LUT-DRC consists of three parts, signal pre-processing unit, data recovery unit, and rate balancing unit.

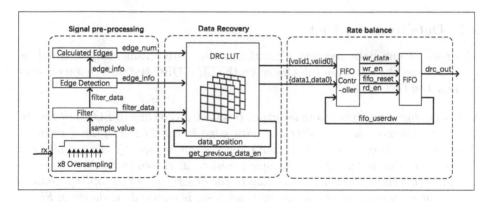

Fig. 1. LUT-DRC system schematic

Signal Pre-processing Unit. It processes the differential input serial data of 125 Mbps in four steps. (1) Oversample the signal by eight times. (2) Filter the oversampled signal to suppress signal interference caused by non-monotonic or overshoot [13]. (3) Calculate the edge position of the current cycle. (4) Calculate

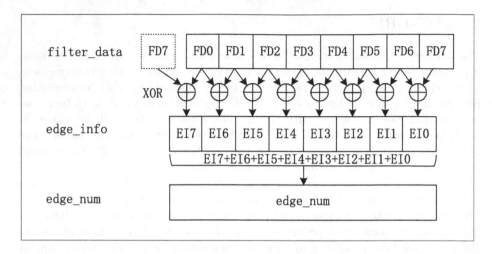

Fig. 2. Schematic diagram of pre-processing mechanism

the number of edges in the current cycle. The schematic of data pre-processing is shown in Fig. 2.

Data Recovery Unit: It recovers data from sampled values based on the output of the signal pre-processing unit and feedback signals from DRC-Table.

Rate Balance Unit: It turns non-homogeneous data streams caused by the clock or data jitter into a homogeneous, uninterrupted data stream.

2.2 Data Recovery Unit

The core of our data recovery algorithm is the DRC Table, implemented by LUTs. We set the following rules based on the LUT-DRC system's characteristics to infer the DRC Table.

1. *Specifying the optimal sample output position: According to BO-CDR theory, the middlemost sample after the data edge is considered optimal recovery data. Therefore, for the x8 oversampling system, we specify the 3rd bit after the data edge as the optimal sample position, as shown in Fig. 3.*
2. *Specifying the setup time: According to the description of the optimal sample output position, a 3-bit wide setup time, Tsu, is required, as shown in Fig. 3.*
3. *Specifying the hold time: For signals, the hold time is generally required to be shorter than the setup time [3,11], so an additional sample interval (1 bit) is required behind the optimal sample output position. Hold time is shown as Th in Fig. 3.*
4. *Specifying the minimum symbol width: Each symbol must be sampled at least five times steadily, according to the setup time and hold time requirements, as shown in Fig. 3.*

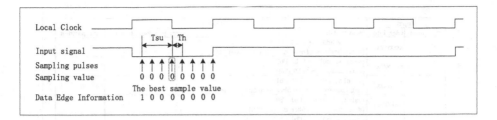

Fig. 3. LUT-DRC Timing Diagram

Infer the possible sampling signal and edge information according to the four rules above.

1. *Two edges in the sampled data: According to rule No.4, each symbol is sampled at least five times. Thus, there must be greater or equal to 4 zeros after each transition edge. Since LUT-DRC uses x8 oversampling, there will be at most two edges and at least one edge per cycle, and there must be at least four consecutive zeros between two edges. Therefore, all six edge-info permutations of the sampled signal with two edges are listed in the edge-num = 2 column, as shown in Fig. 4.*
2. *One edge in the sampled data: Typically, when a clock matches the data rate, a symbol will be sampled eight times in a cycle, and only one edge signal will be generated. The edge position is related to the initial state and may occur at any bit of the sampled value. All eight edge-info permutations of the sampled signal with a single edge are listed in the edge-num = 1 column, as shown in Fig. 4.*

Infer the Residual Flag and Locations of Recovered Data
When the edge is at the lower 0 to 2 bits of the sampled data, the optimal sample position specified by rules No. 2 and 3 is not in the current cycle and will only be output in the next cycle. In such a case, the data corresponding to one edge is left to recover to the next cycle. The formulae for calculating the valid signal of the residual edge and position information are defined by Eq. 2 and Eq. 3.

$$Output\ position\ of\ data\ =\ edge\ position\ -\ 3 \tag{1}$$

$$Residual\ edge\ signal\ =\ (rightmost\ edge\ position\ <\ 3)\ ?\ 1:0 \tag{2}$$

$$Residual\ data\ position\ =\ rightmost\ edge\ +\ 7\ -\ 2 \tag{3}$$

Based on the inferred edge information and Eq. 1 to 3, the DRC Table is designed as shown in Fig. 4. The DRC Table has four inputs: the edge-num and edge-info in the current sampling cycle, the valid signal get-previous-data-en of the residual edge calculated in the previous cycle, and the data-position of the previous edge. The outputs are data1, data0, and their valid bit valid1, valid0 of the current cycle, and the edge information get-previous-data-en and data-position for the next cycle. The data bits and their valid bits are output to the rate balancing unit as recovered data for the current cycle, and the edge residual is fed to the DRC Table as two inputs for the next cycle.

Input		Output		
edge_num	edge_info	recovered data	get_previous_data_en	data_position
0	xxxxxxxx	{valid1,valid0} <= {1'b1,1'b0}; {data1,data0} <= {filter_data[data_position],1'b0};	0	/
	xxxxxxxx	{valid1,valid0} <= {1'b0,1'b0}; {data1,data0} <= {1'b0,1'b0};	0	/
1	xxxxxxxx	{valid1,valid0} <= {1'b0,1'b1}; {data1,data0} <= {1'b0,filter_data[data_position]};	0	/
	10000000	{valid1,valid0} <= {1'b1,1'b0}; {data1,data0} <= {filter_data[4],1'b0};	0	/
	01000000	{valid1,valid0} <= {1'b1,1'b0}; {data1,data0} <= {filter_data[3],1'b0};	0	/
	00100000	{valid1,valid0} <= {1'b1,1'b0}; {data1,data0} <= {filter_data[2],1'b0};	0	/
	00010000	{valid1,valid0} <= {1'b1,1'b0}; {data1,data0} <= {filter_data[1],1'b0};	0	/
	00001000	{valid1,valid0} <= {1'b1,1'b0}; {data1,data0} <= {filter_data[0],1'b0};	0	/
	00000100	{valid1,valid0} <= {1'b0,1'b0}; {data1,data0} <= {1'b0,1'b0};	1	7
	00000010	{valid1,valid0} <= {1'b0,1'b0}; {data1,data0} <= {1'b0,1'b0};	1	6
	00000001	{valid1,valid0} <= {1'b0,1'b0}; {data1,data0} <= {1'b0,1'b0};	1	5
2	10000001	{valid1,valid0} <= {1'b1,1'b1}; {data1,data0} <= {filter_data[data_position],filter_data[4]};	1	5
	10000001	{valid1,valid0} <= {1'b0,1'b1}; {data1,data0} <= {1'b0,filter_data[4]};		
	10000010	{valid1,valid0} <= {1'b1,1'b1}; {data1,data0} <= {filter_data[data_position],filter_data[4]};	1	6
	10000010	{valid1,valid0} <= {1'b0,1'b1}; {data1,data0} <= {1'b0,filter_data[4]};		
	10000100	{valid1,valid0} <= {1'b1,1'b1}; {data1,data0} <= {filter_data[data_position],filter_data[4]};	1	7
	10000100	{valid1,valid0} <= {1'b0,1'b1}; {data1,data0} <= {1'b0,filter_data[4]};		
	01000001	{valid1,valid0} <= {1'b1,1'b1}; {data1,data0} <= {filter_data[data_position],filter_data[3]};	1	5
	01000001	{valid1,valid0} <= {1'b0,1'b1}; {data1,data0} <= {1'b0,filter_data[3]};		
	01000010	{valid1,valid0} <= {1'b1,1'b1}; {data1,data0} <= {filter_data[data_position],filter_data[3]};	1	6
	01000010	{valid1,valid0} <= {1'b0,1'b1}; {data1,data0} <= {1'b0,filter_data[3]};		
	00100001	{valid1,valid0} <= {1'b1,1'b1}; {data1,data0} <= {filter_data[data_position],filter_data[2]};	1	5
	00100001	{valid1,valid0} <= {1'b0,1'b1}; {data1,data0} <= {1'b0,filter_data[2]};		

Fig. 4. LUT-DRC Table

2.3   Rate Balance Unit

FIFO is often used for CDC (Clock Domain Crossing, CDC), data bit width conversion, and data buffering in high-speed serial communications [16]. For example, in the JESD204B protocol, FIFO is used to data align and CDC [14]. In LUT-DRC, the function of FIFO is CDC and data bit width conversion.

FIFO Control Circuit - Write Control Principle. The FIFO write control circuit uses a 9-bit leftward shift register. Valid0 and valid1 signals determine whether we shift data0 or data1, or both into the shift register. For example, suppose valid0 is asserted, then data0 will be shifted into the shift register. Due to the mismatch between the clock and data rate, 2-bit or 1-bit may shift into the shift register per cycle, so we need a 9-bit shift register. When the shift register contains only 8-bit data, we write the lower 8-bit data to the FIFO. Otherwise, we write the upper 8-bit data to the FIFO instead. All cases are shown in Fig. 5.

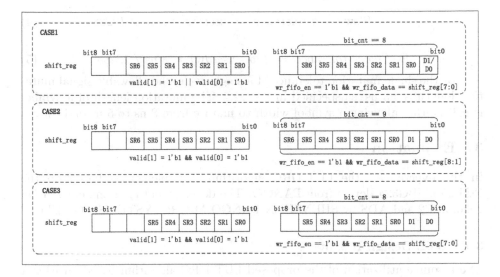

Fig. 5. Rate blance Structure

FIFO Control Circuit - Read Control Principle. The circuitry after DRC requires only 1-bit per cycle and does not allow any interruption in an Ethernet message frame. Otherwise, it will cause RMII (Reduced Media-Independent Interface, RMII) timing recovery errors. Therefore, the FIFO read control module is designed as follows: (1) Reset the FIFO read/write pointer after detecting the JK code in the transmission message. (2) Read FIFO when the userdw signal is equal to the threshold value till the FIFO is empty.

2.4   Anti-jitter Performance of the LUT-DRC

The ability of the proposed LUT-DRC to tolerate persistent slow and fast clock jitter depends on the userdw value in the rate balancing module. For the userdw, having a larger or smaller value is not better. If the value is too small, there is a risk that the FIFO will be read empty, and the Ethernet packet data will be interrupted when the data rate at the sending side is slower than the local clock rate. Suppose the value is too large and the data rate at the sending side is faster than the local clock rate. In that case, there is a risk that the FIFO will be reset by the arrival of a new frame of Ethernet messages before the previous messages read out from the FIFO. Thus the previous frame of Ethernet messages may not be fully recovered. The maximum length of an Ethernet frame is 1.5 kByte, which is 12288 symbols. According to Eq. 4 and 5, when userdw is 48 bits, LUT-DRC has the same resistance to fast and slow clock jitter, allowing the symbol width to be lengthened by 0.0312 ns or shortened by 0.03125 ns, respectively. Such a jitter resistance is multiple times higher than the ±0.00040 ns specified by IEEE 802.3.

$$Slow\ clock\ tolerance\ =\ userdw\ *\ 8\ ns\ /\ 12288 \tag{4}$$

$$Fast\ clock\ tolerance\ =\ (96 - userdw)\ *\ 8\ ns\ /\ 12288 \tag{5}$$

For the single mutation tolerance of a single cycle, the allowable signal mutation length is ±3 ns, as specified in Sect. 2.2. The mutation length of a symbol is ±3 ns, thus allowing a symbol width to mutate from 8 ns to 5 ns or 11 ns.

3 Evaluation

In the experiment, the LUT-DRC algorithm is implemented based on the PGL25-6MBG324 device from PANGO. The development environment is PDS 2020.3.SP2 and ADS by SHENZHEN PANGO MICROSYSTEMS CO., LTD.

3.1 RTL Design Results

The resource utilization of the proposed LUT-DRC algorithm based on FPGA implementation is shown in Table 1. From the table, LUT-DRC utilized only 470 LUT6 and has a low power consumption of 10 mW. The PLL can be shared when multiple PHYs are implemented in the same FPGA, while other resources are related to the number of PHYs instantiated.

Table 1. Resource Utilization and Power

Resource Utilization		
Resource	Utilization	Used for
LUT6	470	RTL Logic
DRAM	1	Rate balance FIFO
APMs	0	–
GPLL	1	x8 oversample clock
IOL	1	x8 oversample
Power		
Total Power		10 mW

3.2   Simulation Results

The simulation results with -0.04 ns and $+0.032$ ns jitter in the transmit clock are shown in Fig. 6 and Fig. 7. When the symbol period is shortened to 7.96 ns or extended to 8.032 ns due to the clock jitter, the DRC at the receiver side can still recover the original data and restore the symbol period to 8 ns. It shows that the LUT-DRC has a higher clock jitter resistance than IEEE 802.3 standard. When the transmitter clock cycle is less or greater than 8 ns, 2 bits or 0 bit data is recovered during this cycle to balance the clock jitter. The data valid signal dout-valid in such case is shown as ② in Fig. 6 and Fig. 7, respectively.

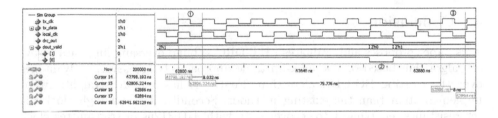

Fig. 6. Fast clock jitter simulation of LUT-DRC

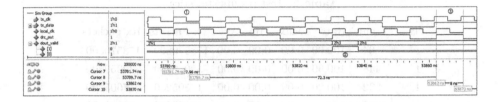

Fig. 7. Slow clock jitter simulation of LUT-DRC

3.3   Test Results

The 100Base-PHY transceiver is implemented based on LUT-DRC, then connected to the network tester and the internal MAC of the FPGA. The test structure is shown in Fig. 8. During the test, the network tester sends 64 Byte, 448 Byte, 832 Byte, 1216 Byte, and 1518 Byte length Ethernet messages to the test board with a minimum frame interval of 96 bits. The data received by the test board will go through LUT-DRC and MAC (Media Access Control, MAC), then loop back to the tester. Results are shown in Table 2.

As shown in Table 2, both the bit error rate and the CRC error rate are zero after transferring $2.5 * 10^8$ packets to the LUT-DRC under the extreme condition specified by the Ethernet data messaging protocol (minimum message spacing of 96 bits, minimum message frame length of 64 bytes, and maximum message frame length of 1518 bytes).

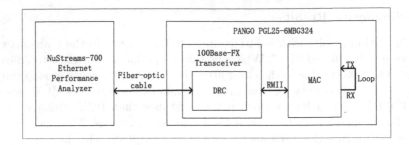

Fig. 8. Test structure

Table 2. Test results statistics

Trial	Frame	Rate	Max	Min	Avg	Tx Packets	Rx packets
1	64	100.00	0.00	0.00	0.00	178570800	178570800
1	448	100.00	0.00	0.00	0.00	32050800	32050800
1	832	100.00	0.00	0.00	0.00	17605200	17605200
1	1216	100.00	0.00	0.00	0.00	12135600	12135600
1	1518	100.00	0.00	0.00	0.00	9752400	9752400

4   Conclusion

This paper proposes and evaluates LUT-DRC, a blind oversampling data recovery algorithm based on the look-up table approach. It has several advantages over the existing BO-CDR algorithm. Firstly, it has a more straightforward implementation than the existing methods. Secondly, it has a high clock jitter resistance, enabling it to recover data with ±0.0312ns of transmitter clock jitter. This performance is higher than the requirements of IEEE802.3 standard. The LUT-DRC was validated on FPGA devices and achieved ideal results with no errors in over 200 million packets of Ethernet messages. Such test results demonstrate that LUT-DRC can be used to implement clock data recovery in FPGAs. We also gives a direct relationship between the clock jitter resistance and the FIFO userdw signal in the LUT-DRC design process. The relationship can provide a certain theoretical calculation basis for the design of DRC in other application scenarios.

References

1. IEEE Standard for Ethernet. IEEE Std 802.3-2018 (Revision of IEEE Std 802.3-2015), pp. 1–5600 (2018)
2. Aggarwal, R.: FPGA place & route challenges. In: Proceedings of the 2014 on International Symposium on Physical Design, pp. 45–46 (2014)
3. Balef, H.A., Jiao, H., de Gyvez, J.P., Goossens, K.: An analytical model for interdependent setup/hold-time characterization of flip-flops. In: 2017 18th International Symposium on Quality Electronic Design (ISQED), pp. 209–214. IEEE (2017)

4. Bushnaq, S., Nakura, T., Ikeda, M., Asada, K.: All digital baseband 50 Mbps data recovery using 5× oversampling with 0.9 data unit interval clock jitter tolerance. In: 2009 12th International Symposium on Design and Diagnostics of Electronic Circuits & Systems, pp. 206–209. IEEE (2009)
5. Xilinx Datasheet. Artix-7 FPGAS data sheet: DC and AC switching characteristics v1. 18 (2015)
6. Defossez, M.: LVDS 4x asynchronous oversampling using 7 series FPGAS and ZYNQ-7000 ap socs. Xilinx Inc. (2017)
7. Cyclone V Device Handbook, vol. 1, Device Overview and Datasheet (2012)
8. Hsieh, M., Sobelman, G.E.: Architectures for multi-gigabit wire-linked clock and data recovery. IEEE Circ. Syst. Mag. **8**(4), 45–57 (2008)
9. Ismail, K., Ismail, T., Mostafa, H.: Design and implementation of CDR and SerDes for high speed optical communication networks using FPGA. In: 2016 18th International Conference on Transparent Optical Networks (ICTON), pp. 1–3. IEEE (2016)
10. Kim, J., Jeong, D.-K.: Multi-gigabit-rate clock and data recovery based on blind oversampling. IEEE Communications Magazine **41**(12), 68–74 (2003)
11. Kim, K.-C.: Measurement of setup and hold time in a CMOS DFF for a synchronizer. J. Korea Inst. Electron. Commun. Sci. **10**(8), 883–890 (2015)
12. Lin, Y.H., Tu, S.H.L.: Implementation of an oversampling data recovery receiver for serial link communications. In: Seventh International Symposium on Signal Processing and Its Applications, vol. 1, Proceedings, pp. 613–616. EURASIP; IEEE; IEEE French Chapter, Paris, France, 01–04 July 2003
13. Gao, N., Zhang, Z., Fang, Y., Guo, Y., Liu, L.-L.: The implementation of a high-performance blind oversampling clock data recovery circuit. Microelectron. Comput. **31**(6), 137–140 (2014)
14. Saheb, H., Haider, S.: Scalable high speed serial interface for data converters: using the JESD204B industry standard. In: 2014 9th International Design and Test Symposium (IDT), pp. 6–11. IEEE (2014)
15. Sugimoto, N., Fukushima, S., Sakai, Y., Oguchi, K., Akatsu, Y.: A small optical Ethernet PC card for fiber-to-the-notebook pcs and its applications. In: Optical Transmission, Switching, and Subsystems II, vol. 5625, pp. 491–497. SPIE (2005)
16. Sung, G.-M., Tung, L.-F., Wang, H.-K., Lin, J.-H.: USB transceiver with a serial interface engine and FIFO queue for efficient FPGA-to-FPGA communication. IEEE Access **8**, 69788–69799 (2020)
17. Yang, C.-K.K., Farjad-Rad, R., Horowitz, M.A.: A 0.5-m CMOS 4.0-Gbit/s serial link transceiver with data recovery using oversampling. IEEE J. Solid-State Circ. **33**(5), 713–722 (1998)

Network Services

Research and Implementation of Importing Distributed Cluster Data into Cloud Platform Based on JMS

Junyuan Zheng[1]($\boxtimes$), Hongtao Ni[1], Min Sun[1], and Xinjian Chen[2]

[1] Suzhou City University, Suzhou, China
zhengjunyuan@szcu.edu.cn
[2] Soochow University, Suzhou, China

Abstract. This project researches and implements the problem of concurrent data repeated submission during the integration of distributed cluster system to a cloud platform. In this paper, three different solutions are proposed. Through analysis and comparison, the JMS service provided by Weblogic, which has an automatic failover function, is selected as the final solution to prevent concurrent duplicate data submission. And this solution only takes little code change effort on the existing system. When different users select duplicate records for concurrent submission, the message queue function of the Weblogic JMS service is used to record the records to be submitted. At the same time, the duplicate records are removed to avoid the problem of concurrent duplicate submission. Finally, the records can be imported in to the corresponding cloud platform through WebService technology.

Keywords: Distributed Cluster · Weblogic JMS · Cloud Platform · Concurrent and Repeated Submission · WebService

1 Introduction

With the rapid growth of the system service volume, the traditional single-machine deployment mode is unable to meet business needs. At this time, distributed cluster deployment mode arises [1]. Multiple services are deployed on various servers, and each service is a node. This way, when N nodes are deployed, the business processing capacity is increased by N times. The collection of these nodes is called a cluster. The cluster environment is a good choice for improving the business processing capacity [2]. A PLM product in this project is a cluster system deployed on Weblogic. However, with the further development of Internet technology, more and more systems are migrating to the cloud. Compared with most prefabricated data centers, the cloud platform is cheaper, more stable, more secure, and more scalable. This project is to import the data in a PLM system into the Oracle fusion PD cloud platform. So this paper mainly introduces the asynchronous message processing technology based on JMS [3] to prevent different users in the distributed cluster system from selecting duplicate records for concurrent submission and import.

© ICST Institute for Computer Sciences, Social Informatics and Telecommunications Engineering 2023
Published by Springer Nature Switzerland AG 2023. All Rights Reserved
S. Yu et al. (Eds.): TridentCom 2022, LNICST 489, pp. 73–83, 2023.
https://doi.org/10.1007/978-3-031-33458-0_6

2 Core Terms

2.1 JMS

Middleware is a software technology between client and server [4], message middleware is a middleware technology composed of message transmission mechanism or message queue mode [5], and Java Message Service (JMS) is a specification proposed by Sun company to unify various information middleware interfaces, which provides a set of interfaces independent of specific implementation [6], which is used to connect two application programs, or send messages in a distributed system. JMS is a vendor-independent API that performs asynchronous communication to access, send, and receive system messages. Because the data transmission process is not synchronized [7], the message sender can send a message without waiting for a response. The message sender sends the message to a virtual channel (queue or topic), and the message receiver listens to or subscribes to the channel. The message may eventually be forwarded to one or more message receivers, who do not need to respond to the message sender [8]. The use of Weblogic JMS can be divided into two parts. One part is that Weblogic publishes the corresponding JMS service as a server to provide services for the client program. The other part is that the application publishes messages as a client to the JMS server or obtains statements from the JMS server for consumption [9].

2.2 WebService

WebService is the interaction between network applications based on the HTTP protocol through the Internet. It uses WSDL (Web service definition language) and soap (simple request protocol) to realize the call between different languages [10]. WebService is a network-based, distributed, and modular component. It performs specific tasks and complies with detailed technical specifications. These specifications enable WebService to interact with other compatible components. It mainly uses HTTP and soap protocols to transmit business data on the web. Soap invokes business objects through HTTP to perform remote function calls; Web users can use soap and HTTP to call remote objects through methods called by the Web [11].

3 Method

3.1 Scheme Demonstration and Selection

This project realizes the system integration function of a PLM system to the fusion cloud platform. This PLM product has a DFCO object that needs to be imported into the item object in the fusion cloud system. The project schematic and other files uploaded by the user under the publish workspace tab on the DFCO object, such as .DRW files and .PRT files, users can search and select an item number in the fusion cloud platform system as the corresponding item object to be imported. After clicking publish, the complementary relationship between the two can be imported through WebService, and the files will also be imported synchronously. When importing objects with attachments such as engineering schematics, due to the size of the attachment capacity, the import takes a specific time (usually a few seconds). At first, it is set to import only a single piece of data at a time. Because the import time of a single record is short, the problem of repeated submission can be ignored. The customer feels that the efficiency is too low in the process of using, so the system must select several records to import simultaneously. However, if multiple records are submitted together, the submission processing time will be longer, and it is easy for multiple users to submit duplicate records concurrently. That is, user a is submitting 1 and 2 records in DFCO1, but the submission has not been completed. User B also selects duplicate records in DFCO1 for submission because there are duplicate data in them, which will lead to the problem of data duplication and confusion.

According to the needs of customers, three solutions were studied and designed during the development of this project. The solutions and comparison are listed as below:

Scheme 1: Creating a static array list. Because the static array list is stored in the method area of the Java virtual machine, the elements contained in the method area are always unique in the whole program and are shared by all threads; it is very appropriate to judge duplicate records [12]. All DFCO ID numbers submitted in this project can be put into this static array list before submission. When another user submits, the selected ID number will be compared with this static array list. If there are no duplicate records, the ID number submitted by the user will also be added to this static array list. If one or more identical ID numbers exist in the static array list, a warning message will pop up to tell the user that duplicate records are in the submitted data. Duplicate records will not be submitted, but only non-duplicate records will be submitted. After completing the submission, delete the corresponding ID number from the static array list. This solution has no problem for single-machine systems. However, the PLM system of this project is a distributed cluster system deployed on Weblogic. The distributed cluster system is composed of one admin node and one or more slave nodes, and the PLM system is deployed on each node, so there will be a static array list on each node; that is, there will be multiple static arrays lists exist at the same time, and the DFCO ID submitted on different nodes will only exist in the static array list on the corresponding node. Multiple static arrays lists cannot be compared to obtain duplicate records. Therefore, this solution can not play a role in comparison and deduplication for distributed cluster systems.

Scheme 2: The popular message queues rabbitmq, rocketmq, and ActiveMQ [13] are used to control the submitted records through message queues. This method checks whether the same ID number exists in the message queue before submitting records in batch. If it does not exist, the ID numbers of the records to be submitted are all stored in the message queue, and then the records are taken from the message queue one by one and synchronized to the fusion cloud System one by one. Suppose the record ID to be submitted and the ID in the message wise are found to have duplicate records through comparison. In that case, a warning message will pop up to tell the user that there are duplicate records in the submitted data. Duplicate records will not be submitted. Only non-duplicate records in the message queue will be submitted. Because there is only one message queue in the distributed system, this solution can meet the requirements of the distributed cluster system. However, to prevent the repeated submission of such a small function, the jar package of the corresponding message queue needs to be additionally introduced. At the same time, the service of a message queue needs to be deployed and maintained. The big code changes need a lot of effort. Moreover, the import function is highly dependent on the message queue service; Once there is a problem with the message queue service, the import function cannot be used. The coupling is too strong, and no backup message queue is available.

Scheme 3: As this PLM product is deployed on Weblogic, Weblogic has very powerful functions as an application server [14]. It has its own JMS service. Users can configure the JMS service to realize the function of the message queue. The JMS function is similar to scheme two's working principle of the message queue and will not be described here. In this scheme, the code changes are minor. Meanwhile, Weblogic has the functions of redundant backup and automatic failover when the server where JMS is located (usually the admin node) goes down, it will automatically change one of the slave nodes into a new admin node. At the same time, move all services to the new admin node (including the configured JMS service). In this way, the system can be ensured to have high availability in the actual project application; It can also play the role of data disaster recovery backup.

Through the comparison of the above three schemes relying on static array list, third-party message queue, and Weblogic's built-in JMS service, it can be seen that scheme three can solve the problem of repeated data submission with minimal changes in the existing technology and successfully realize the import of cloud platform data. Therefore, this solution is selected for this project.

3.2 System Design and Implementation

The specific architecture block diagram of the project system is shown in Fig. 1.

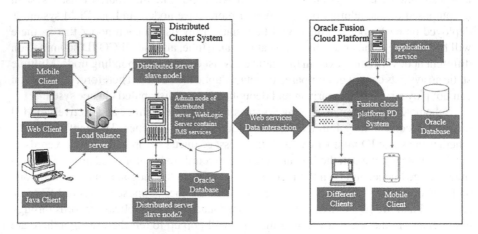

Fig. 1. System architecture block diagram.

The PLM distributed cluster system of the project is shown in the left block. It is composed of a load balance server, admin node, and multiple slave nodes, which are deployed on the WebLogic Server [15], and the JMS service is deployed on the admin node. The right block is the Oracle fusion PD cloud platform system. This distributed cluster system integrates data through WebService to import data to Oracle fusion cloud platform.

The above system architecture diagram shows that the JMS service is only deployed on the admin node, it is unique in the distributed cluster system. It can be used to record the submitted data and perform deduplication. When different users perform the publish action, that is, data migration, the ID corresponding to the selected data in the database will be put into the JMS message queue for queuing. Because the ID of each data in the database is unique, each time the newly submitted data ID is put into the message queue, it will be compared with the existing data ID in the JMS message queue. If there is a duplicate data ID, the duplicate data ID will be discarded, and only the non-duplicate data ID will be added to the JMS message queue for subsequent migration. After completing the data migration, remove the corresponding data ID from the JMS message queue. The problem of concurrent duplicate submission is avoided by caching the JMS message queue, and then removing the duplicate data ID.

JMS Configuration Method
Parameter Allocation Method
Modifying the Weblogic configuration file on the server side of the corresponding distributed system can realize the role of deploying JMS services on Weblogic. For example, the configuration file path of the distributed server in this project is: $cluster-name/$agile_Home/agiledomain/config/config.xml. Add the following contents to the config.xml file:

```
<cluster>
    <name>$ClusterName</name>
    ...
</cluster>
<jms-server>
    <name>C4cJMSServer</name>
    <target>$ClusterName</target>
    <persistent-store>C4cStore</persistent-store>
</jms-server>
<jdbc-store>
    <name>C4cStore</name>
    <prefix-name>C4C_</prefix-name>
    <data-source>AgileHaDataSource</data-source>
    <distribution-policy>Distributed</distribution-policy>
    <target>$ClusterName</target>
    <migration-policy>Always</migration-policy>
</jdbc-store>
```

After restarting the server, you can see the JMS server on the corresponding Weblogic console. From the configuration content added above, you can see that the JMS server configured in this project is named C4cJMSServer, as shown in Fig. 2.

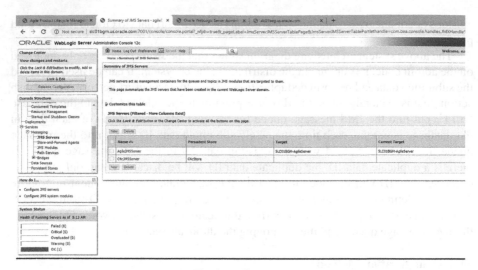

Fig. 2. JMS Server.

Console Configuration Method

In addition to the above method of modifying the configuration file, you can also configure the JMS server through the interface on the Weblogic console. Find the corresponding domain under the domain structure on the left of the Weblogic console, enter the service, and then enter the JMS server under the messaging. Then click the "new" button in the list on the right to enter the navigation page of the new JMS server, and then follow the prompts step by step [16]. The manual configuration method will eventually be written into the configuration file. The effect is the same as the method of modifying the configuration file parameters mentioned in Sect. 2.2.1.1. After the configuration, you can also see the configured JMS service, such as C4cJMSServer on the console.

Cloud Platform Data Import

Weblogic deploys the framework of Java-based WebService. The distributed system and cloud platform exchange data through WebService. The WSDL file of this standard-based interface modular WebService is easy to manage and maintain, and it can ensure compatibility between different clients (.Net, Java, and BPEL). In addition, the batch API access mechanism can provide better access performance.

Before data migration, the user can map the data to be migrated to the item object of the cloud platform by modifying the parameters of the configuration properties file on the distributed system side. For example, a parameter can be defined CLOUD_ CAD_ INTEGRATION_ ENABLED, the value of this parameter can be set to be true or false to enable or disable this import function, and through the parameter CLOUD_ INTE-GRATION_ APPLICATION_ APINAME = OracleCloud and CLOUD_ PD_ ITEM_ REF_ OBJECT_ SUBCLASS_ APINAME = PDItem to control the API interface of the corresponding application. Define the WebService objects that can be queried, accessed, and operated in the WSDL file of the cloud platform. For example, the item object in the cloud platform in this project is shown in Fig. 3.

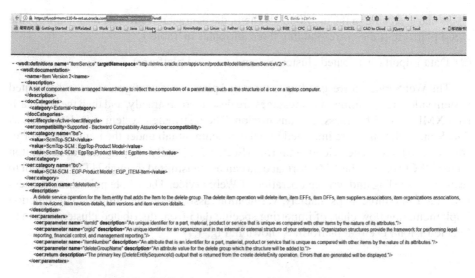

Fig. 3. WebService access item object configuration.

Then, build the jar file generated by compilation and put it into the distributed system server. At the same time, import the Keystore in the WSDL file of the cloud platform's WebService into the distributed system. Only in this way can the access be trusted. The WebService operations are mainly divided into 2 steps: (1) Search and query functions. The distributed cluster system accesses the cloud platform system, and the cloud platform query data in the distributed cluster system. (2) Data import. This step import data from the distributed cluster system to the cloud platform. The two detailed steps analysis are as follows:

(1) Search query function (cloud platform -> distributed cluster system)

On the distributed system side, you can query the item object of the cloud platform defined by the WSDL file to be operated. At the same time, you can map the attribute in the distributed system to be migrated with the attribute of the corresponding cloud platform's WebService, as shown in Table 1.

Table 1. Attribute relation correspondence table.

Reference object attribute	Webservice attribute
Name	ChangeNotice
Description	Description
Current Status	StatusTypeValue

When searching in the distributed system, the data search attribute returned from the cloud platform is the corresponding three attributes in Table 1.

(2) Data import (distributed cluster system - > cloud platform)

The WebService corresponding to the cloud platform is configured on the distributed system side, the operations and messages are described abstractly, and then the standardized XML is used for message transmission. The distributed system side data, such as .DRW and .PRT files, are imported into the attachment tab under the item object corresponding to the searched cloud platform in Sect. 3.2.2 (1). By clicking the Publish button on the DFCO object, the XML format data can be transmitted through HTTP protocol to realize the reading and writing operation of WebService. The whole publishing process is divided into three steps, namely, verification, association, and import. The function implementation flow chart of importing specific data from distributed cluster system to Oracle fusion PD cloud platform is shown in Fig. 4.

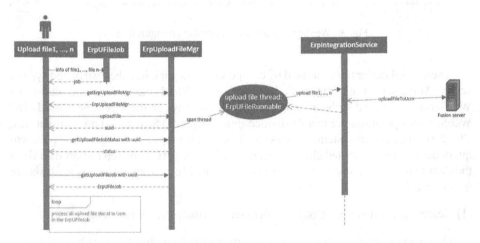

Fig. 4. Data import flow chart.

4   Results

After the system is implemented through the above scheme, creating a new DFCO00029 object at the distributed cluster system side, and adding the attachment files P00003.PRT and P00003.DRW under this object. Then, there are two attachment files P00003.PRT and P00003.DRW which designed by the CAD drawing software under the publish workspace tab of the DFCO00029 object in the distributed system. Configuring the JMS service and WebService with this paper's solution on the Weblogic. After that, the DFCO00029 object to associated Oracle fusion Cloud platform, we can see the results as shown in Fig. 5.

Analyzing Fig. 5, it can be seen the two attachment files P00003.PRT and P00003.DRW associate the "Item Number" field with the item object "pd_itemtest6 and pd_itentest110" of the fusion cloud platform through the WebService technology in Sect. 3.2.2 of this paper.

Fig. 5. Distributed cluster import interface.

At the same time, migrate the two records P00003.PRT and P00003.DRW to the oracle fusion cloud platform. If another user logs in to the distributed cluster system through other clients and submits the imported records (P00003.PRT and P00003.DRW) repeatedly, the warning message "selected row (s) is being published and cannot be added to a new job. Selected rows not being published will be added to a new job" will popup on the user interface as shown in Fig. 6, duplicate records will not send to the JMS message queue, which plays a role in preventing duplicate submission.

DFCO00029

DFCO00029   Pending
DFCO

| ○ Comment | ➔ Next Status ▾ | ⧉ Navigator | Actions ▾ |

| Cover Page | Affected Files * | Publish Workspace * | Workflow | Relationships * | Attachments | History |

⚠ Selected row(s) is being published and cannot be added to a new job. Selected rows not being published will be added to a new job.

Publish Workspace

| Un-Relate item | Un-Relate ECO | Validate | Publish | Refresh |

✓	Folder Number	Folder Description	Folder Version	Item Number	Item Description	Item Lifecycle Phase
	P00003.PRT	PRT0001-PRT	1	pd_itemtest6	pd_itemtest6	Design
	P00003.DRW	DRW0001-DRW	1	pd_itentest110	pd_itentest110	Design

Fig. 6. Duplicate data submission warning.

After the distributed cluster system prompts the import completely, you can see all the item objects just imported under the "change order" object corresponding to the Oracle fusion cloud platform. The relationship has been successfully imported, as shown in Fig. 7.

The corresponding records (attachments P00003.PRT and P00003.DRW) successfully imported to the corresponding items in the cloud platform, the attachment record P00003.PRT is shown in the pd_itemtest6 of the Oracle fusion cloud platform, as shown in Fig. 8.

Fig. 7. Import the item object of the cloud platform.

Fig. 8. Import file of item object.

5   Conclusions

This paper proposes a specific implementation method of importing distributed cluster data into the cloud platform based on Weblogic JMS and WebService technology. When importing data, the problem of duplicate submission of concurrent data is effectively prevented through Weblogic JMS. The scheme provided in this project is used to migrate the cloud platform of the actual project, which can effectively and accurately realize the data import function and prevent the problem of duplicate submission of concurrent records. Through this method, users can meet the actual application requirements of importing the data and information on the products of the distributed cluster system to the cloud platform, which not only saves the development cycle but also is easy to realize, thus significantly improving the production efficiency and quality of the software.

References

1. Wu, G.-F., Ding, J.-H., Xu, Y.-B.: Distributed data synchronization based on JMS. Comput. Syst. Appl. **24**(01), 171–175 (2015)
2. AN, B., MA, J., CAO, D., et al.: Towards efficient resource management in virtual clouds. In: 2017 IEEE 37th International Conference on Distributed Computing Systems Workshops(ICDCSW) on Proceedings, pp. 320–323. IEEE, Atlanta (2017)
3. Luo, X.-B., Dong, S.-B., Xu, H., Zhang, L.: Asynchronous message processing technology and application based on JMS. Comput. Eng. 2002(12), 121–122+149 (2002)
4. Wang, L.-L., Xiao, C.-J., Zhang, X.-W.: A message-oriented secure transmission middleware model. Comput. Sci. **2007**(07), 288–292 (2007)
5. Li, Y.-M., Ling, J.: Design of security message middleware. Comput. Eng. Design **32**(06), 1934–1937 (2011)
6. Deng, Y.-K., Wang, C.: Research and design of JMS-based secure communication model. Comput. Eng. Design **30**(15), 3526–3530 (2009)
7. Shang, X.-N., Sun, L.-Y., Peng, T., Liu, C.: Design and research of a secure communication scheme for asynchronous network system. Comput. Eng. Sci. **34**(11), 34–37 (2012)
8. Zheng, L., Chen, Y.-L., Liu, R.-M., Zheng, D.-Y.: Research on cloud service of message queue based on open source. Inf. Commun. Technol. Policy **311**(05), 52–56 (2020)
9. Zheng, J.-Y.: Implementation of PLM product WebService access on oracle cloud platform. Comput. Knowl. Technol. **15**(07), 37–39 (2019)
10. Tan, Y.-J.: Research on java message communication. Comput. Program. Skills Mainten. **414**(12), 40–41+61 (2019)

11. Peng, X.-T.: The design and realization of electronic document archiving interface based on XML and JMS. In: 3rd International Conference on Advanced Education Technology and Management Science (AETMS) on Proceedings, pp. 418–422. Science and Engineering Research Center, Beijing (2016)
12. Liu, J.-C., Xavier. R.: An array content static analysis based on non-contiguous partitions. Comput. Lang. Syst. Struct. 47, 104–129 (2017)
13. Zhang, J., Man, S.-G., Liu, K., Zhou, L.-J.: Using message queue to achieve data consistency method. Comput. Syst. Appl. **28**(09), 185–189 (2019)
14. Ni, H.-T: Deployment of Web project on ORACLE cloud platform. Wirel. Internet Technol. 15(06), 18–19 (2018)
15. Somogyi, A., Revanuru, N., Irudayaraj, R., Felts, S., Zhou, T., Zhao-Perez, F.: Patent issued for system and method for using a gridlink data source to connect an application server with a clustered database. US20120066363 A1, US (2015)
16. Elim168 blog page. https://blog.csdn.net/elim168/article/details/72674355. Accessed 21 July 2022
17. Su, Z.-F.: Research on heterogeneous database integration scheme based on Open URL protocol and XML Schema. Comput. Eng. Design **29**(16), 4308–4310 (2018)

Mobile ad HOC Networks

Design of a 5G Experimental Platform Based on OpenAirInterface

Quentin Douarre[1,2], El-Mehdi Djelloul[1], Pascal Berthou[3], Daniela Dragomirescu[2], and Philippe Owezarski[1(✉)]

[1] LAAS-CNRS, Université de Toulouse, CNRS, Toulouse, France
owe@laas.fr
[2] LAAS-CNRS, Université de Toulouse, INSA, Toulouse, France
qdouarre@insa-toulouse.fr, daniela@laas.fr
[3] LAAS-CNRS, Université de Toulouse, UPS, Toulouse, France
berthou@laas.fr

Abstract. 5G has been designed for providing the appropriate services for a large range of applications requiring high throughput, low latency, a support for the IoT, or for Industry 4.0 business, etc. One of its strong statements is the sofwarization of most of its functions for providing more flexibility, and a support that can easily evolve for providing new services. In that context, OpenSource implementations of 5G functions arise. One of this implementation is the 5G OpenAirInterface (OAI). This paper then describes how a 5G experimental platform taking advantage of the 5G OAI software suite was designed and deployed at LAAS-CNRS. The aim of the platform is to be as generic as possible for being able to experiment and evaluate all 5G new mechanisms and protocols issued from researchers. This paper then specifically addresses how the compatibility issues between 5G OAI and the equipments (USRP, servers, operating systems, etc.) were fixed. The paper also proposes a performance evaluation of the 5G OAI platform and analyzes its limits.

Keywords: 5G · Experimental platform · network softwarization · OpenAirInterface

1 Introduction

Over the last few decades, several major evolutions impacted network design, as a huge number of new usages and applications requires wireless and mobile communications: smart-phones, IoT, vehicular networks, etc. This lead to the arising of multiple wireless technologies for local networks (Wifi, ...), long distance cellular networks (4G, 5G, ...), for the IoT (Sigfox, LoRA, ...), etc. Wireless networks present many limits nowadays because of the hertzien nature of the transmission support that provides only limited capacities compared with wired communication supports, together with a huge variability of available communication resources. Providing the multiple services requested by current applications in such a context is a tricky challenge.

© ICST Institute for Computer Sciences, Social Informatics and Telecommunications Engineering 2023
Published by Springer Nature Switzerland AG 2023. All Rights Reserved
S. Yu et al. (Eds.): TridentCom 2022, LNICST 489, pp. 87–103, 2023.
https://doi.org/10.1007/978-3-031-33458-0_7

Providing theses multiple Qualities of Services (QoS) on wireless and mobile networks is a hot topic that the 3GPP standardization organization is strongly considering nowadays, especially for 5G. The old monolithic architecture of "One-size-fits-all" kind passed away, and a service oriented one has to replace it. Network slicing is the main aspect for developing such architecture. A network slice is defined by 3GPP as a virtual network that provides the characteristics of a specific network. In other words, each Mobile Network Operator (MNO) splits its physical infrastructure in several slices dedicated to several service providers, as a slice for automotive, and another one for the health domains, etc. Thus, each slice could be devoted to a specific professional domain with its own QoS requirements. When a user equipment (UE) registers on the network, it then has to use a slice id to connect to the appropriate slice. Up to now, 3GPP standardized three kinds of slices/services: Enhanced Mobile Broadband (eMBB), ultra-reliable low latency (URLLC) and massive internet of things (mIoT). eMBB service provides high throughput, URLCC provides low latency communication for real-time applications/services, and mIoT is specifically dedicated for IoT services. Implementing slicing approach however requires high flexibility and programmability for 5G networks. It then takes advantage of the network softwarization approach, as NFV (Network Function Virtualization) and SDN (Software Defined network) paradigm. The first approach provides the flexibility of NF (Network function) thanks to virtualization, and the second one separates the control and data planes. Several prototypes based on NFV and SDN have already been proposed for the slicing in core networks (CN) [1] and the radio access network (RAN) [2].

5G also benefits from the analyses of previously deployed networks by operators and equipment manufacturers. The cost of updating or managing hardware devices when it is required to add new services for instance is dramatically high. In that context also, network softwarization provides strong advantages as updating or replacing some functions implemented in software (NFV) can be made remotely, and without any action on the hardware. Network management then becomes more flexible and cheaper. That's why the opensource market has decided to take an interest in the telecommunication sector under many aspects such as USRP or mobile networks. Several projects are born to propose 4G or 5G opensource implementations.

In this context, the research community takes advantage of this network virtualization aspect as it is then possible to assess their research proposals not only using simulator, but also by direct software implementations that can be rapidly integrated on the actual market networks. For this purpose, LAAS-CNRS lab in Toulouse, France decided to design and implement such a 5G experimental platform. This paper describes its design principles and first evaluation results. For that it takes advantage of the concepts of Software defined Radio techniques (SDR) and the open-source software OpenAirInterface (OAI) platform for the experimental assessment of 5G wireless networks.

The rest of this paper is as follows: Sect. 2 gives a short presentation of the elements of a software 5G platform, as OAI, required for implementing our 5G experimental platform. Section 3 details the equipments required for setting up our 5G platform. It also mostly presents the software components that have been included, as well as the way they have been configured. This Sect. 2 also indicates how to fix the main encountered problems during the installation and configuration of such a platform, in order to provide an important document for engineers or researcher that would be interested in setting up such a platform for their own researches. Then, Sect. 4 shows some performance results gained on our 5G experimental platform. It especially illustrates the performance cost of using a 5G software platform. It can be seen as the "price" of flexibility, compared to the old fashion monolithic hardware only networks. Finally, Sect. 5 concludes this paper.

2 The 5G Opensource Platform

2.1 5G Standalone Architecture

There are several 5G network architectures. The 5G Non-Standalone architecture builds on existing LTE infrastructures such as ENB and EPC. It is therefore a kind of 4G++. The architecture we are interested in is the 5G-NR Standalone which characterizes the new generation of mobile networks. It is composed of several elements, each having a specific role. They are arranged as depicted on Fig. 1:

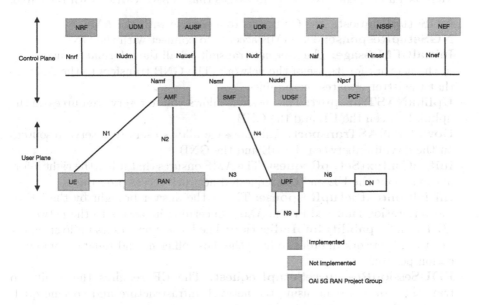

Fig. 1. 5G-NR Standalone Architecture

The UE represents the User Equipment. It is a connected object like a smartphone, a connected watch or a drone. At first, on our 5G experimental platform, it will be a Dell server. But it will be replaced later by a Google Pixel 6 cell-phone. Its radio interface communicates with the core network RAN. In 5G, this operator equipment is called a GNB. It represents the entry point to the provider's network. Next comes the AMF. It is in charge of the good management of the registrations on the network, the handovers and the maintenance of the client databases. The SMF, the UPF and the UDM are responsible for the PDUsessions allowing to identify a communication and to fix the "rules" of transmission. The NRF controls the virtual functions of the network. It is essential, because in recent years the importance of virtualization as a research topic clearly appears. The AUSF takes care of the authentication of the users of the 5G network. It interacts closely with the AMF and UDM. The UDR centralizes detailed customer information such as their subscription. To finish with this little tour, there is the NSSF. This component of the core network supervises the management of slicing.

2.2   NGAP Protocol

During the design of this 5G experimental platform, the NGAP protocol proved to be the most important one. This protocol is in charge of the control plan between the GNB and the AMF. Thanks to it, we can see the inscriptions on the network, the reservations of resource in Uplink and Downlink, the request for PDUsession, etc.

Here is a non-exhaustive list of messages that NGAP carries with their role:

- **NGSetupRequest:** The GNB asks to associate with the AMF
- **NGSetupResponse:** The AMF accepts to connect with the GNB
- **InitialUEMessage:** The user has transmitted all the information necessary to the network for its use of the network. The GNB transfers to the AMF so that the latter updates these tables
- **UplinkNASTransport:** This message allows you to reserve resources on the uplink between the UE and the GNB
- **DownlinkNASTransport:** This message allows users to reserve resources on the downlink between the UE and the GNB
- **InitialContextSetupRequest:** The AMF ensures that it has the right information about the UE and the requested network access procedures.
- **InitialContextSetupResponse:** This is the answer brought by the UE to the verification launched by the AMF concerning its access to the network
- **UERadioCapabilityInfoIndication:** The UE announces its radio specificities to the network in order to have the most efficient and reliable communication possible
- **PDUSessionRessourceSetupRequest:** The UE requires the ability to transmit a data stream using the network infrastructure and specific quality of service parameters.
- **PDUSessionRessourceSetupResponse:** The SMF says that it has the capacity to make the reservation by respecting the parameters setting requested by the UE

The above messages indicate that the attachment of the device to the network is successful. With the help of Wireshark, it is possible to check the good registration of the UE on the 5G network, the reservation of the resources and the good transfer of the data. This tool designed for sniffing the packets in transit on the network provides a great help to researchers and network managers.

2.3 The Main Communication Channels

The 5G standard defines several different types of communication channels. The following lists them in a non-exhaustive way, useful for understanding the rest of the report and possibly debugging errors.

- **PBCCH** (Packet Broadcast Control Channel): Control information and signaling related to packet services.
- **PCCCH** (Packet Common Control Channel): Includes logical channels for GPRS common control signaling. These sub-channels include: PRACH (Packet Random Access Channel), PPCH (Packet Paging Channel), PAGCH (Packet Access Grant Channel) et PNCH (Packet Notification Channel).
- **PDCCH** (Physical Downlink Control Channel): Consists of a set of resource elements that carry data from higher layers to the physical layer or from the physical layer to higher layers.
- **PRACH** (Physical Random Access Channel): An uplink channel used by the UE for connection request. The PRACH is used to transport data from the RACH transport channel.
- **PUSCH** (Physical Uplink Shared Channel): Used to transmit the uplink shared channel (UL-SCH) and L1 and L2 control information.
- **PDSCH** (Physical Downlink Shared Channel): A transport channel used for the transmission of user data, dedicated control and user-specific upper layer information and downlink system information.

2.4 The OAI 5G Project

The OpenAirInterface project is led by the OSA. Its objective is to implement future opensource cellular networks in order to demystify the inner workings of these networks and to make it easier for the global research community to contribute to their development.

OpenAirInterface 5G is divided into three main projects: 5G RAN, 5G Core Network and Mosaic5G. Mosaic5G adds a range of virtual functionalities to the network and proposes, in addition to the data and control planes, a management plane. However, Mosaic5G will be stopped in favor of a new project called Trirematics which will have the same objectives using more modern technologies to achieve them.

The first two projects are the ones we are particularly interested in. 5G RAN deals with the interactions between the UE and the GNB. It thus focuses on the lower layers of the OSI model.

Several architectures are supported, as depicted on Fig. 2. The one we are interested in is the standalone one. The project is still evolving. Soon, RAN slicing and Massive MIMO, two fundamental features of theorized 5G, will be supported. 5G Core Network offers the management of the almost complete architecture of the 5G-NR Standalone, the highest level of functionality. In order to create all components virtually, Docker is used. As with the previous project, this one continues to be developed. Missing components like UDSF, AF will be coded (see Fig. 1 for more information about missing components), slicing management will be added in version 1.4, etc.

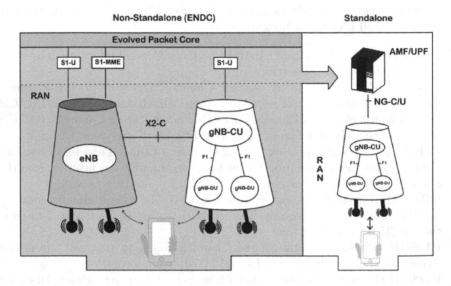

Fig. 2. Interactions, according to the chosen architecture, of the radio entities of the network

3   OAI 5G Installation Steps on Dell Servers and Google Pixel 6

This section describes the installation and configuration of the 5G experimental platform, based on OAI. This platform consists of a 5G Core Network (CN), a gNB and a UE. After describing the hardware required for the installation of the platform, the following parts will be dedicated to the installation steps of the different modules of the 5G network.

Interested readers can refer to a more detailed report for this 5G platform [3].

3.1   Material Required

The configuration chosen for the platform is as follows:

- The gNB and the CN are installed on the same machine
- The UE is installed on a second machine

Each machine is connected to a USRP to act as a radio module.
The couple (gNB+CN) is installed on the machine 1:

- A Dell Precision Rack 7920 18-core server
- An Ettus B210 (or X310) USRP connected via USB 3.0 (or 10G-Ethernet)
- Two broadband log-periodic antennas (850 MHz–6.5 GHz)

Regarding the UE on machine 2:

- A Dell Precision Rack 7920 18-core server
- An Ettus B210 (or X310) USRP connected via USB 3.0 (or 10 Gb/s Ethernet)
- Two broadband log-periodic antennas (850 MHz–6.5 GHz)

3.2 Software Configuration

Each Dell Precision Rack 7920 server must have the following features:

- Ubuntu 20.04 LTS
- Lowlatency kernel to download
- Disable C-States and P-States (except C0 and C1 which allow the cores to run at full speed but also to be able to stop in case of interruption)
- Disable CPU hyperthreading
- Configure each core as Governor Performance
- Specialize the cores manually according to the tasks

To download the low latency kernel for Ubuntu 20.04 LTS, enter the following command:

sudo apt-get install linux-image-lowlatency linux-headers-lowlatency

To be able to configure the CPUs operation correctly, the i7z package is needed. It allows the return of detailed information about the operation states.

sudo apt-get install i7z
sudo i7z

Now go to the BIOS to leave only the C0 state (operation at the maximum energy of the CPUs) and C1 for the stop of the CPUs (interrupts). When the servers are launched, press F2.

Then configure all the cores in performance mode: mode allowing to use the full computing power of the CPUs. First, install the cpufrequtils package which will allow changing the power consumption of the CPUs, and the operating frequencies.

Recommendation: We recommend using a USRP x310 for the gNB + CN part configured as 10 Gb ethernet. For this, at least a category 6 cable must be used.

Installation and Configuration of USRP. The installation and configuration of the USRPs are done by following the *Getting Started Guides*, available on the Ettus Research website at the following address:
https://files.ettus.com/manual/page_usrp_x3x0.html.

Installation of the 5G Network Core on Machine 1. On the machine, once the OS is installed, the chosen USRP must be configured. Ideally, for gNB+CN, a powerful USRP capable of handling a 10 Gb/s throughput is needed. For this, the Ettus X310 USRP is ideal, but the B210 could work as well.

Installation of the gNB on Machine 1. The main prerequisite for the installation of the gNB is the installation of UHD. This driver allows the management of the USRP.

Installation of the UE on Machine 2. For the UE, machine 2 is associated with a USRP (B210) that must be installed and configured on the machine. It is advised to install the core on machine 2, allowing to symmetrize the roles of machines 1 and 2.

Then, on machine 2, it is enough to take again the installation of the gNB whose argument --nrUE installs the modules required for launching the UE.

NB: We have chosen to install the UE on the machine with the gray background and the GNB + heart network on the colored background.

Configuration of New Bands. To configure new bands, go to the folder: /openairinterface5g/targets/PROJECTS/GENERIC-NR-5GC/CONF

It contains some models made for several bands working with the USRPs b210 and x310 from Ettus. Between the two USRP models, there are differences in the way they are configured. For creating other configurations, these models can serve as a basis.

During the configuration, several very important parameters need to be modified according to the band. For example:

- absoluteFrequencySSB
- dl_frequencyBand
- dl_offstToCarrier
- dl_carrierBandwidth
- initialDLBWPlocationAndBandwidth
- initialDLBWPcontrolResourceSetZero

The list goes on. The uplink band has to be configured the same way. At the bottom of the configuration files are the tx and rx attenuation, the gains which are essential parameters for the good configuration of the USRP and for the good management of the available radio resources.

To help configure some of the settings, refer to the two sites: https://5g-tools.com/5g-nr-gscn-calculator/ https://www.sqimway.com/nr_refA.php

NB: It is essential to start from a valid GSCN to find the corresponding ARFCN.

It is also possible to go to the file nr_mac_common.c to see the configurations entered in the code.

3.3 Debugging Phase

IMPORTANT: The use of Wireshark is highly recommended to follow the exchanges between the different entities and to detect errors or missing NGAP exchanges. Go to the demo-oai interface. Set it up by filtering all exchanges containing NGAP.

Communication Problem Between gNB and CN

1. Make sure the tracking area code is set to 1
2. mcc = 208 et mnc = 99 (MCC identifies the country, MNC identifies the operator)

NB: The changes are mainly in the gNB configuration but also a little in the core configuration.

Problems of Identification of the UE

1. Ensure the consistency of the core record tables and the information passed to the UE.
2. Check in the configuration of the UE:
   - dnn = "oai";
   - nssai_sst = 1;
   - nssai_sd = 1;

NB: This setting is recommended on the gNB side because it is the one that is directly implemented in the core network. For selecting another one, change the initial CN configuration in the file **/oai-cn5g-fed/docker-compose/docker-compose-basic-nrf.yaml**

Ping Problems Between the UE and the GNB

1. Make sure that the identifier of the UE is well contained in the files of the databases oai-db, oai-db1, oai-db2
2. Make sure that on Wireshark, the NGAP packet PDUSessionRequest is sent so that the UE is assigned an address.

DNS Problems Core Network

1. Change DNS to:
   - DEFAULT_DNS_IPV4_ADDRESS = 127.0.0.53
   - DEFAULT_DNS_SEC_IPV4_ADDRESS = 8.8.8.8
2. Add these lines in the core network configuration in the file **/oai-cn5g-fed/docker-compose/docker-compose-basic-nrf.yaml** for the UDM and UDR:
   - REGISTER_NRF = yes
   - NFR_IPV4_ADDRESS = 192.168.70.130
   - NFR_PORT = 80
   - NRF_API_VERSION = v1
   - NRF_FQDN = oai-nrf

Problem Launching the gNB with the USRP x310 Configuration.
Sometimes, the launching of the program crashes with an abort message. Just
restart it to make it work again. This is a stability problem in the OpenAirInterface code that has not yet been fixed.

3.4 Google Pixel 6 Settings

First of all, SIM cards and their reader are required in order to be able to
configure the phones correctly. All required information can be found at the
following address: https://open-cells.com/index.php/sim-cards/.

Then change the firmwares of the phones so that our network is visible and
it becomes possible to connect using the European 5G bands (n28a, n41, n78).
The procedure for installing new firmware is described here:
https://developers.google.com/android/images
Install the firmware **12.1.0 (SQ3A.220705.001.B1, Jul 2022,
EMEA/APAC carriers)**.

Then, go into the advanced settings of the phone. To do this, go to the phone
application, enter *#*#4636#*#*, then choose NR-only.

At the same time, to program a SIM card, first download the Opencells uicc
program.

IMPORTANT: At the imsi level, a MCC of 001 and a MNC of 01 must
be entered. The key of the telephone and the operator can be found in the
databases of the core network. We have already programmed for 6 UE. They
use the following imsis: 001010000000001, 001010000000002, 001010000000003,
001010000000004, 001010000000005, 001010000000006.
NB: Remember to turn off the wifi so to easily connect to the 5G platform

On the side of GNB, it is necessary to change for each configuration the MCC
to 001 and MNC to 01. This because the operators restrict the configurations
with a MCC of 208 indicating France that would not make possible some tests
out of the operator networks.

On the core network side, keep the SQL databases oai_db and oai_db2 up
to date. Install sqlite and mysql on the servers to do this. The databases are
already configured to host 6 different UE. The only thing to change is the SQN
of the last 4 UE according to the value indicated during the configuration of
the SIM card. For the 001010000000001 and 001010000000002 the configuration
is already done. It is then necessary to modify the .yaml file called at the time
of the launching of the heart to make appear the good values of the MCC and
MNC in the various places.

3.5 5G Experimental Platform Galery

This section aims at illustrating with a pictures gallery how the 5G experimental
platform looks like, with additional comments on the pictures to explain what
equipment implements what component (Figs. 3, 4, 5 and 6).

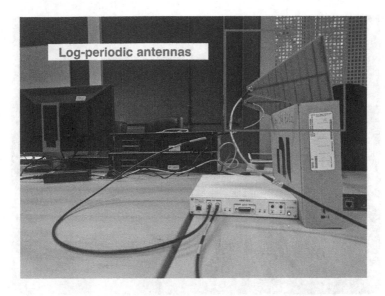

Fig. 3. Log-périodic antennas operating on the 850 MHz–6.5 GHz band

Fig. 4. Dell Precision Rack 7920 serveurs

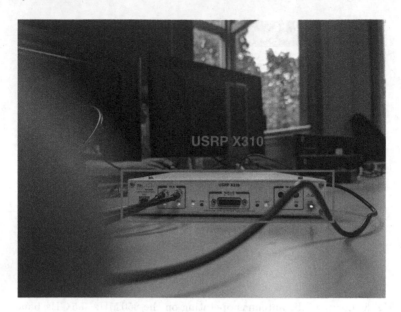

Fig. 5. Operating USRP X310

4 Experimental Evaluation

4.1 Simple IPerf Tests

In order to evaluate the performances of our 5G experimental platform, the IPerf tool was selected for generating and transferring packets. IPerf is a software tool for transferring IP packets from a source to a destination machines. In our case, we selected to transfer packets downlink from gNB to the UE.

Figures 7 and 8 show the evolution of the transfer throughput according to time. Two frequencies bands have been considered. The experiment makes the size of data to transmit and the bandwidth vary. The size of the data to transmit is noted N, the bandwidth is noted B. Frequencies bands considered are the n41 band whose central frequency is 2.5 GHz, and n78 band whose central frequency is 3.5 GHZ. These two bands have been selected as they are the most used ones, currently.

iPerf Results on the n41 Band - 2.5 GHz
Figure 7 shows that the transfer of small size packets, on a limited bandwidth, perfectly works. The theoretical throughput of 0.1 Mbits/s is reached.

Fig. 6. LAAS' 5G OAI experimental platform

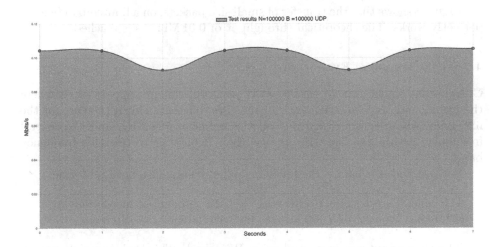

Fig. 7. Throughput on the n41 band with $N = 0.1\,\text{Mbits}$ and $B = 0.1\,\text{MHz}$

iPerf in n78 Band - 3.5 GHz

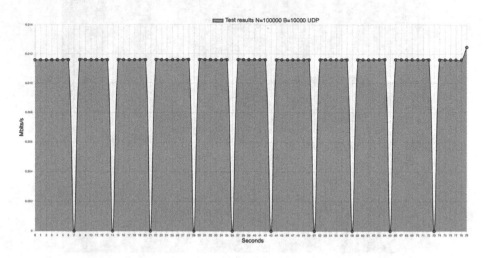

Fig. 8. Throughput on the n41 band with $N = 0.1$ Mbits and $B = 10$ kHz

Figure 8 shows that the transfer of small size packets, on a limited bandwidth, perfectly works. The theoretical throughput of 0.01 Mbits/s is reached.

4.2   File Transfers Evaluation

Current implementation of the 5G OAI platform cannot support cases where the uplink and downlink frequencies bands are different. This is the case for the n28 band whose central frequency on the uplink is 722 MHz, and the central frequency downlink is 780 MHz. It was then impossible to test this frequency band.

For n41 and n78 bands, the following experiments have been performed:

- n41 band: Transfer of a 100 Mbytes file with throughput measurement
- n78 band: Transfer of a 100 Mbytes file with latency measurement

The throughput was measured using Wireshark. This tool does not provide directly the latency measurement, but a simplifying hypothesis that was used consists in considering the latency as the half of the Round Trip Time (RTT). RTT is the time for a packet to go to the destination and going back to its source.

The throughput and latency measurements obtained for the transfer of the 100 MBytes file are given in Table 1.

Table 1. Performance indicators for the transfer of a 100 MBytes file on bands n41 and n78

	Débit moyen	Latence moyenne
n41 band	7.3 Mbits/s	21.2 ms
n78 band	9.3 Mbits/s	15.5 ms

The results were expected: when the frequency increases, the throughput increases as well, and the latency is reduced. The 3GPP norms indicate optimal throughputs of 10 Gbits/s for the eMBB slice, and an optimal latency of 1 ms. It was impossible on our platform to reach such values by a high degree of magnitude.

This can be explained by several factors:

- The limited emission power of our antennas (as we are in the public domain, we are not allowed to generate 5G signals that could interfere with the commercial 5G services).
- In the public domain in which the experiments took place, the environment is uncontrolled: there is a significant noise and frequent interferences from the commercial cellular networks.
- Our servers appear to have too limited computing power.

4.3   Experiments with the Google Pixel 6 Smartphone

With the Google Pixel 6 connected to our 5G OAI network, it was possible to tun the following tests and applications:

- Sending and receiving of e-mails
- Have an access to the Internet
- Perform audio and video streaming

In an empirical way, Fig. 9 illustrates that the use of the Google Pixel 6 smartphone with the 5G OAI network is very smooth, with the possibility of viewing several Internet pages simultaneously. Concerning the streaming, it was possible to view a 4K video.

Fig. 9. The Google Pixel 6 gets Internet access through the 5G OAI network

5   Conclusion

5G has been designed for providing the appropriate services for a large range of applications requiring high throughput, low latency, a support for the IoT, or for Industry 4.0 business, etc. One of its strong statement is the sofwarization of most of its functions for providing more flexibility, and a support that can easily evolve for providing new services. At that time, the commercial 5G services are far from providing all the 5G promises, 5G operators just providing with their 5G networks more throughput for the users than a 4G network. The softwarization process is at its early age, and OAI is certainly the most advanced 5G software platform nowadays. As explained in this paper, 5G OAI is far from being completely developed and debugged. It was however possible to deploy a 5G experimental platform in our lab. This was a 6 months long study of the OAI documentation, OAI debugging, and OAI testing. But, as a result, our platform works, at least for simple services. For instance, the modules for 5G slicing are not available yet. The use of the smartphone is satisfactory with current applications, and with a single user. That is the limit of the current 5G OAI. The performances with all the softwarized components are limited compared to 5G objectives. That's what our evaluation experiments exhibited. The current limit is mostly due to the computing power of our servers. Let us recall that our servers are very powerful compared to computer standards: they have 18 cores, large RAM, large communication buses, etc. Computing power would be today the cost of network flexibility.

For this reason, a significant effort has to be provided for optimizing the codes, but also by optimizing some of the normalized 5G mechanisms and protocols. This is the case for instance for 5G resources allocation [4]. Optimizing 5G mechanisms and protocol is part of our future works. We will also increase the size of the platform in order to be able to create several cells with several UEs in each of them. Last, the platform will be moved in an anechoic room to allow us to generate more powerful signals, and for avoiding being impacted by external noise and interferences.

References

1. Qazi, Z.A., et al.: A high performance packet core for next generation cellular networks. In: ACM SIGCOMM (2017)
2. Foukas, X., et al.: Orion: RAN slicing for a flexible and cost-effective multi-service mobile network architecture. In: ACM MobiCom (2017)
3. Douarre, Q., Djelloul, M.: The 5G in Opensource: Installation of an experimental Platform using OpenAirInterface 5G. LAAS report, September 2022
4. Oussakel, I., Owezarski, P., Berthou, P., Houssin, L.: Toward radio access network slicing enforcement in multi-cell 5G system. J. Netw. Syst. Manage. (JNSM) **31**, 8 (2022)

MEC Application Migration by Using AdvantEDGE

Prachi Vinod Wadatkar[1,2]($\boxtimes$) ⓘ, Rosario G. Garroppo[2] ⓘ,
and Gianfranco Nencioni[1] ⓘ

[1] Department of Electrical Engineering and Computer Science,
University of Stavanger, Kjell Arholms gate 41, 4021 Stavanger, Norway
{prachi.v.wadatkar,gianfranco.nencioni}@uis.no
[2] Department of Information Engineering, University of Pisa,
Via Girolamo Caruso, 16, 56122 Pisa, Italy
rosario.garroppo@unipi.it

Abstract. Multi-access Edge Computing (MEC) and 5G are key technologies for the development of new applications requiring low latency and for computation off-loading. Emulation tools, such as AdvantEDGE, allow to rapidly test new services and resource management techniques in the 5G-MEC infrastructure. The paper presents an experimental study aimed to show the usage of AdvantEDGE tool for evaluating the migration performance of a MEC application. The key aspect of the study is that the application mobility is obtained by using the migration of the Kubernetes (K8s) application pod. The standard K8s does not have the ability to support the pod migration in a cluster of nodes. While recent research proposes a mechanism to migrate pod, there is no work investigating the migration technique with the AdvantEDGE MEC solution. Referring to a video service, the paper shows a scheme developed during the experimental study to allow the pod migration when K8s is used with AdvantEDGE. Using the emulation of user mobility given by AdvantEDGE platform, the described experimental tests allow to show the performance of the MEC application migration.

Keywords: Multi-Access Edge Computing (MEC) · AdvantEDGE · 5G-MEC Emulation · Kubernetes · Migration

1 Introduction

Due to the increasing demand for computational and Internet of Things (IoT) applications, the fifth generation (5G) of mobile networks will face unusual traffic volume. At end-users, computing-intensive applications become an inherent concern due to the end user's limited storage and computational abilities. Multi-access Edge Computing (MEC) is the emerging technology in the 5G network that can process a large amount of data within the Radio Access Network

This work was supported by the Norwegian Research Council through the 5G-MODaNeI project (no. 308909).

ⓒ ICST Institute for Computer Sciences, Social Informatics and Telecommunications Engineering 2023
Published by Springer Nature Switzerland AG 2023. All Rights Reserved
S. Yu et al. (Eds.): TridentCom 2022, LNICST 489, pp. 104–118, 2023.
https://doi.org/10.1007/978-3-031-33458-0_8

(RAN) [1]. European Telecommunications Standards Institute (ETSI) provides the MEC specifications to meet the requirements of the applications where real-time processing is needed. The core idea of MEC is to deploy the cloud computing capabilities within the RAN, close to the end-user [2]. ETSI MEC Ecosystem [3] refers to the MEC solutions that support the experimentation and deployment of the practical scenarios that include a 5G-MEC framework. In those MEC solutions, a recent study [4–8] shows AdvantEDGE as a potential emulation platform tool to perform the different challenges in the MEC framework.

AdvantEdge [9] is a Mobile Edge Emulation Platform (MEEP) that runs on Kubernetes (K8s) [10] and Docker [11]. The emulation platform enables the analysis with edge computing technologies, applications, and services. AdvantEdge provides the ability to explore edge deployment models, and allows the user to modify the deployment scenarios considering elements such as network topology, network characteristics, application mobility, and UE movement. AdvantEdge provides the connection of real cloudlet and UE applications so that simulation can capture the impact of network design on application performance. AdvantEdge also allows the measurements collection in InfluxDB time series [12]. InfluxDB is a time series database built specifically for storing time series data.

Virtualization technologies support the deployment and management of the MEC applications and the MEC host (MEH). K8s is developed by Google [13] and is a superior technology for automating the management, scalability, and deployment of containers and nodes. Containers are prevalently used for running stateful applications. However, the standard K8s don't have an in-built mechanism to migrate the stateful containers from one node to another.

The main contribution of the paper is the description of an experimental testbed aimed at evaluating the performance of MEHs migration strategies using the 5G-MEC emulation scenario implemented by the AdvantEDGE platform. Then, referring to a video streaming application, the paper presents an experimental analysis of the application migration in the runtime mode. The different time-related parameters related to the migration process are presented and analysed.

The paper is organized as follows. Section 2 gives the ETSI MEC application migration use case and the standardized ETSI MEC API for the application mobility using the AdvantEDGE platform. Section 3 presents the related work, while Sect. 4 discusses the main advantages of AdvantEDGE and the emulated network scenario considered for the experimental tests. Section 5 shows the testbed setup, the integration of the application migration techniques, and the working strategies. Section 6 evaluates the average values and confidence interval (CI) over the observation period of selected time-related performance parameters. The future work and the conclusions are summarized in Sect. 7.

2   Background

ETSI has specified the management of the MEC by considering the system level, the host level and the network layer functionalities. MEC Orchestrator (MEO) is the brain and has the overall view of the MEC system level management elements. The MEC system level consists of the MEHs, physical resources, applications and its services along with system topology. The MEO is the responsible entity for selecting the MEH during the application instantiation for the end user. In the ETSI MEC architecture, a MEH has a MEC Platform (MEP), which can establish a connectivity with the other MEPs by using the Mp3 reference point. Mp3 reference point is the platform-to-platform interface that exchanges the information related to the application mobility between MEHs. In a disturbed deployment of the MEC system, multiple instances of the MEC application can be present and maintain the connectivity over different MEHs. The entities in the MEC application mobility within the intra-MEC system scope are presented in [14].

For the MEC application mobility, there are two entities to focus on: the application availability in the target host and the user context transfer. In the first entity, the application is required to be available in the targeted MEH, where the targeted MEH does not have designated application to provide the service to the end user. The MEO decides the application instantiation on the targeted MEH and has the ability to download the application image. The MEO can initiate the application by using the Virtualization Infrastructure Manager (VIM). After the application availability at the targeted host, a communication link is established to transfer the user context as the end user application is connected to the MEC application, the end user is not expected to be aware of the application mobility and the deployment of the application along with its state. A MEC stateful application needs to deliver the service continuity by importing the user context from the source MEH to the targeted MEH.

AdvantEDGE provides a support to the ETSI MEC API of the application mobility and allows the integration with the network scenario [15]. The API provides the support for relocation of user context between MEHs but the application instance relocation is not supported. The use case allows the MEC application user context transfer by using the API. The end-user devices are tracked and subscribed to the mobility procedure where the mobility manager receives the mobility notification of the end-user movement and the MEC application mobility. For running the application mobility experiment, the automation support is provided by AdvantEDGE for the User Equipment (UE) movement and the Point of Access (PoA) mobility.

3   Related Work

In [16], the authors discuss mobility-related issues, mainly focusing on the best instance to migrate the MEC application and what content to migrate to improve the Quality of Experience (QoE). Different mobility factors are taken into consideration. The work in [17] shows the optimal way to migrate the MEC application and the complete migration strategies to reduce energy expenditure. In [18], the authors consider the prototype system approach at the network layer to manage a seamless connection between the edge server and the mobile devices.

Some of the works carried out the experimental tests using different MEC model, and migration strategies, one of them presents K8s as the MEO [19]. The work proposes reactive service migration with the evolved packet core (EPC). Other experimental studies present the integration of Open Source MANO (OSM), an orchestrator, with Open Network Edge Services Software (OpenNESS) [20], a MEC platform, to migrate the MEC applications between MEHs [21]. The study includes two components, one to maintain the application's state with the client and the other to focus on management.

In [22], the authors discuss various container and migration strategies focusing on the fog, edge, and cloud; the work focus on the current approaches and the framework for container-based services migration. In [23], the authors describe different methods of the migration of pod in K8s and present the results of downtime with and without migration along with the data size transferred. For stateful container migration, a prototype approach using an extended version of kubelet and customized containers is available on GitHub [24]. The prototype approach provides an extension of the *kubectl* command that includes a command for the checkpoint and migration of the running pod in K8s. This work presents the running pod migration across single or multiple clusters and adds the function necessary to the pod migration. Furthermore, the prototype implementation includes pod migration operator at control plane that has custom resource and the controller.

4 Emulated Network Scenario

AdvantEDGE platform is a MEEP that provides emulated and experimental environment with edge enabling technologies [25]. The platform runs on Docker and K8s, and provides experimentation with MEC deployment models along with their applications and services. AdvantEDGE supports some of the APIs and the edge services standardized by the ETSI MEC such as ETSI MEC 013 Location [26], ETSI MEC 012 Radio Network Information [27], ETSI MEC 028 WLAN Information [28], ETSI MEC 011 Edge Platform Application Enablement [29] and ETSI MEC 021 Application Mobility [14]. In addition to that, AdvantEDGE allows the changes of the location of devices within the network using their own APIs. The platform allows network characteristics configuration such as latency, jitter, throughput and packet loss that can be applied to the scenario. During the scenario deployment, containers run in the K8s pod. In each deployed pod, AdvantEDGE includes an companion container called as sidecar. The role of the sidecar is to apply the network characteristics from the simulation model. To implement simulation model, *TC-engine* is the responsible micro-service, *tc* is called as Traffic Control. Whereas *tc-netem* technology is used for the network characteristics in each sidecar. AdvantEDGE supports different edge application and client deployment model. Furthermore, the platform allows mobility event, UE movement and mapping the geo-location of each elements. The UE movement can be monitored and visualized using the Geospatial Subsystem.

Figure 1 shows the emulated network scenario based on AdvantEDGE platform. The scenario consists of one UE (ue1) in zone1, whereas zone2 and zone3 include an emulated MEHs edge1 and edge2 respectively along with PoAs. There are three different network access technologies representing different zones. The ue1 is able to connect to the MEHs via PoAs within each zone depending on the ue1 movement. The blue boxes are the MEHs. The brown boxs represent the mec-app for MEC application deployed on edge1 and vlc1 for ue1. The green box is the physical UE. The antennas represent the PoAs. Initially the MEC application runs on the MEH edge1 connected to a point on the network called Zone2. The edge1 MEC application and services are running externally to the platform. AdvantEDGE provides support to integrate the external MEC application and services within the scenario using an IP address and the port number. The zone elements represent a subnet, which can be composed by a set of network elements offering traffic transport service. Since the MEC architecture can be applied to any network technology, it is necessary to assume that further network elements are interposed between the infrastructures of an Internet Service Provider (ISP) and the edges of the network. These network elements are enclosed in logical zones and are not simulated by AdvantEDGE. In the Fig. 1, Operator1 is the ISP, which in the considered network scenario, provides the IP connectivity through the three access technologies and the IP services supported by means of the MEC architecture.

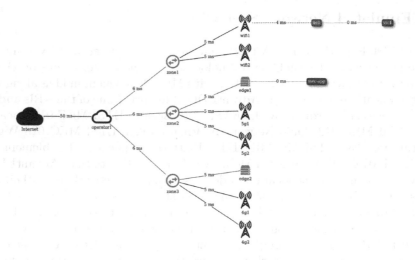

Fig. 1. Network scenario described by the AdvantEDGE GUI (Color figure online)

AdvantEDGE platform supports to allocate the physical locations of each elements presented in the scenario. The three different PoAs networking technologies are mapped in different geographical locations. Reference to the geographical scenario is in the Fig. 2. The scenario is an Arno River area in Pisa. The scenario considers three different access technologies: 4G, 5G and WiFi. The coverage radius of WiFi access technology is 200 m (in red), whereas is 500 m and 1000 m for 5G (in orange) and 4G (in blue) respectively. In the figure, the blue line denotes the ue1 path considered for the experimentation.

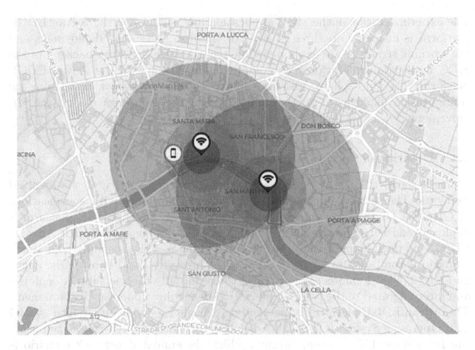

Fig. 2. Map of the scenario considered in the experimental analysis with AdvantEDGE platform. (Color figure online)

The value of each metric of the determined optimum path between the MEH and the UE, as a function of the chosen PoA, are summarized in Table 1.

Table 1. Parameters of the path for the experimental tests

MEH-UE	WiFi-1	4G-1	5G-1	WiFI-2	4G-2	5G-2
PLoss (%)	0	0.016	0	0	0.0079	0
Jitter (ms)	12	16	13	16	15	17
Latency (ms)	26	31	30	26	39	30

The GIS API (getGeoDataByName) was utilized during the tests to gather data on the geographical locations of the network's devices. These statistics make it possible to determine the client-to-PoA distance, which is critical to identify the set of PoAs that can provide connectivity to the client. AdvantEDGE's Sandbox API (sendEvent) enables runtime PoA handover, which permits switching the PoA to which the client is connected.

5   Experimentation

The experimentation of the MEC application migration using the AdvantEDGE platform is divided into three phases. In the first phase, the deployment and the working structure are explained. The second phase deals the backend of the MEC application migration technique and integration with the AdvantEDGE platform. The third phase presents the experiment's migration flow, from the configuration deployment to the completion of the migration during the UE movement.

5.1   Description of the Testbed

Figure 3 shows the testbed overview with logical connectivity of the involved elements. The testbed is composed of 3 physical machines with specifications of GIGABYTE (32/512) Intel i7 NUCs. The NUC1 AdvantEDGE platform is deployed and runs the emulated network scenario implemented with Advant-EDGE and the UE application. As described in the Sect. 4, the emulated network scenario is composed by a set of APs, with three areas and two MEHs, edge1 and edge2. NUC2 enforces edge1 MEH where initially the mec-app is deployed and later migrated to the NUC3 edge2 MEH depending upon the UE movement. The AdvantEDGE platform is installed on a single K8s node on Ubuntu 20.04.4 LTS Operating System (OS). The AdvantEDGE platform GUI is accessed using the IP address 152.94.64.68, through which the emulated network scenario is configured and deployed. In the scenario configuration, the external mec-app is mapped with the edge1 mec-app using the IP address and the port number, called the external node integration. AdvantEDGE provides support for experimenting with external nodes and applications.

The management and deployment of the edge1 and edge2 MEHs are done using the cluster of K8s nodes: edge1 functions as the master node and edge2 as worker node. The MEHs interact with the AdvantEDGE platform using the API request and response provided by the AdvantEDGE platform. AdvantEDGE supports some of the ETSI MEC APIs. In particular, the location API, standardized by the ETSI GS as MEC 013 [26], is used to track the information related to the UE physical location in the network during the experimentation. The mec-app is a video streaming application in a container deployed using K8s. The K8s run the application and allow access to the service using the IP address and port number. As the mec-app is deployed on the edge1 MEH, the video streaming is always accessed through the edge1 IP address and the specified

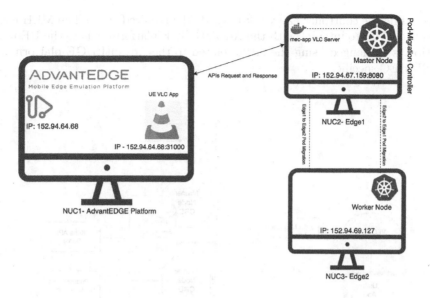

Fig. 3. The testbed

port number, as shown in the Fig. 3. The UE application is a VLC application [30] running on the NUC1. The UE application reaches the mec-app video streaming service through AdvantEDGE. The mec-app service maps within the AdvantEDGE platform, where AdvantEDGE creates a mec-app and UE app pod using the external node integration.

5.2 Migrating MEC Application

The MEHs edge1 (master node) and edge2 (worker node) form a single cluster of nodes using K8s as depicted in Fig. 4. In the single cluster, edge1 deploys the mec-app, a video streaming pod. As initially in the emulated network scenario, the UE is connected to edge1; during UE movement mec-app is migrated to edge2. The single cluster node using the extended K8s version prototypical implementation is available on GitHub [24]. The prototype implementation includes components such as the K8s, containerd-cri with the extensions of CRIU, which is needed for runtime pod migration and podmigration-operator. The K8s insures the node synchronization within the cluster of nodes. The extended version of the K8s provides *kubectl-migrate* and *kubectl-checkpoint* commands [24]. In addition, edge1 is configured as the NFS server, whereas the worker node is the NFS client. The NFS shared folder results into giving access to the edge1 checkpoint storage where the mec-app is running. The pod migration API server directs the pod migration from edge1 to edge2 or vice-versa. The podmigration controller includes Customized Resource Definition (CRD) and a custom controller to watch the pod migration within the cluster of the nodes. CRD is a mechanism that supports user-defined data types in K8s and permits to design the required state while the controller can work towards the required state. The MEH edge1 runs the script to interact with the AdvantEDGE platform, where the UE information is exchanged using the APIs related to the AdvantEDGE platform and ETSI MEC specific.

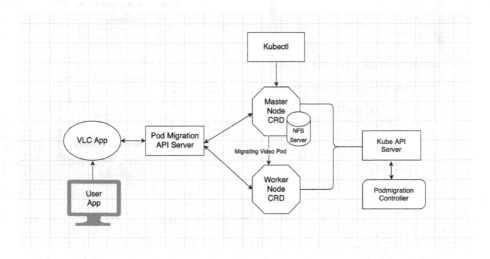

Fig. 4. Video pod migration

5.3   Migration Flow

Figure 5 presents the workflow of the MEC application migration between two MEHs using the AdvantEDGE platform. The emulated network scenario is created, configured, and deployed using the AdvantEDGE platform GUI. As soon as the scenario is deployed, AdvantEDGE creates a mec-app and UE app (referred to as vlc1) pod, which allows the UE app to reach the mec-app service via AdvantEDGE. The manager (script) registers the scenario information and the location of PoA and UE using the API. Initially, as configured in the scenario, vlc1 is closest and connected to the edge1 node. The vlc1 is connected, and the data is routed to the mec-app via edge1. The manager has pre-configured zone coverage for edge1 and edge2 depending upon the PoAs base station location. A PoA mobility event occurs during the UE movement, and the manager registers the UE location closer to the edge2. The manager orchestrates the scenario and guards the coordination with the podmigration-controller. The manager triggers and instructs the podmigration-controller for the mec-app migration from edge1 to edge2. The podmigration-controller starts the migration and checks if the source pod on edge1 is running or not. The podmigration-controller capture and contain the container state in a pod. Once source pod running information is acquired, a checkpoint of the source pod is created at the edge2 along with the checkpoint path. The edge2 confirms the checkpoint info creation; then, the pod is restored at edge2. The edge2 informs podmigration-controller if the new pod is running or not. Once a new pod is running, vlc1 establishes the connection with the mec-app now running on edge2 via the manager. Later, the manager terminates the source pod with the help of the podmigration-controller. The manager affirms the app information with the UE application. In Fig. 5, the total migration time is noted from the start of the checkpoint to the completion of the migration process, whereas downtime is accounted for by resuming the pod on the destination MEH.

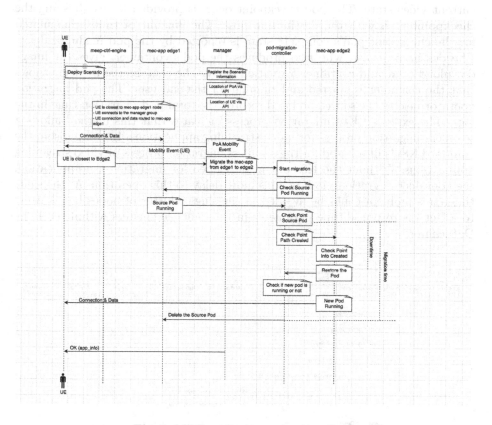

Fig. 5. MEC application migration flow

6 Experimental Results

The test aims to determine the pod migration capabilities of the extended K8s and the different time-related performance parameters. Figure 6 summarizes the different time-related parameters that can be measured during the experimental sessions. Furthermore, the observed values during only one migration are reported in the bottom line. The shown results refer to the video streaming application migration with the extended migration techniques. The test reports that the average MEC application migration time value is 3.762 s. The start of the delay is noted between the manager (script) to the pod migration operator. The start config delay mentioned in Fig. 6 relates to collecting information about running pods, such as whether the source pod is running or not and the current video state. The pod checkpoint delay is provided for establishing the checkpoint path with the destination host. The amount of time accumulated for the checkpoint pod's complete state is reported by the pod readiness delay. The destination host, who also produces the pod's container, gives the image download delay and container formation delay. The container start delay shows that the container is started and running for the end user. The pod migration operator deletes the source pod and records the total pod migration time in the logs. The extended K8s migration process indicates that this method allows a seamless migration process for video streaming applications. In comparison, the standard K8s is ill-advised for the seamless migration process of video streaming applications. Without the K8s plugin developed for migrating the application, the container migration via K8s adds more delay to this operation. At the same time, this problem could be avoided in the single cluster of nodes but is likely to affect the response time parameter in the multiple clusters within the Edge Datacenter.

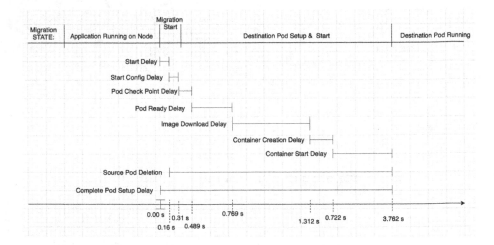

Fig. 6. Migration process in edge K8s

Table 2. Description of time measured in the experiments.

Δ (ms)	Total time taken for the application migration
Δ_1 (ms)	Time taken by the manager to start the migration
Δ_2 (ms)	Time accumulated for the Source Pod Checkpoint.
Δ_3 (ms)	Time for the Pod Ready Delay
Δ_4 (ms)	Time to restore the Pod at destination

Table 3. Time measurements (Averaging 100 independent migration executions)

	95% C.I.	Median	Min	Max	95-th percentile
Δ (ms)	3015.46 ± 134.533	2866.5	1459	6789	3903.7
Δ_1 (ms)	19.4857 ± 1.1836	18.0	10	35	29.0
Δ_2 (ms)	8.1714 ± 0.6100	8.0	4	16	13.0
Δ_3 (ms)	7.971 ± 0.6087	7.0	14	16	12.549
Δ_4 (ms)	2995.371 ± 112.016	2860.0	2230	4471	3688.65

A more deep analysis has been carried out observing a large set of migration events. In particular, these experimental tests are carried out between the two MEHs on the defined UE path as shown in Fig. 2. A total 100 number of migrations were taken place to observe the average migration time over the period. The extended version of the K8s and the NFS sharing helped to achieve a better and stable application migration latency. The MEC application migration time was noted from the pod migration operator logs with the help of the Kube API server. The time recorded in the logs depicts each stage of the pod migration from the creation of the checkpoint till the source pod's deletion. For the network layer, flannel is used. In K8s, the flannel supports the layer 3 networks between the multiple nodes across the single cluster, removing the port mapping complexities and providing the end user with a seamless migration experience.

Table 2 presents the set of time-related parameters that can be obtained from the K8s log, using the pod migration operator. The timeline dictate migration of the pod in the single cluster of nodes i.e. MEHs. Table 3 reports the statistical values of the Table 2 parameters during the experimental tests. The reported values refer to the statistics estimated observing 100 pod migration executions. Figure 7 shows the mean and the 95% CI of the total migration time taken by the pod migration operator, as a function of the considered number of pod migration executions. The figure points out the large CI when only 10 migrations are observed. In this case the values are ranged from 2.7 s to 4.5 s. On the contrary, after the observation of 100 migrations, the 95% C.I. has a size of only 134.53 ms around the mean value.

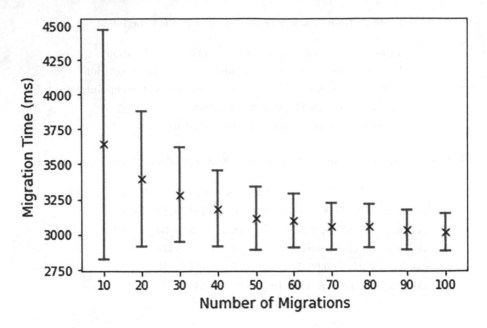

Fig. 7. Confidence interval of MEC application migration

7 Conclusion

In this paper, we presented and studied a scenario to migrate the MEC applications by using K8s and AdvantEDGE. The experimental study presents an analysis of the MEC application migration by using the extended K8s pod migration strategies. We evaluated the pod migration strategies for the MEC applications and the time related to the pod migrations between MEHs.

Acknowledgment. This work was partially supported by the Norwegian Research Council through the 5G- MODaNeI project (no. 308909) and the Italian Ministry of Education and Research (MIUR) in the framework of the FoReLab project (Departments of Excellence).

References

1. Pham, Q.V., et al.: A survey of multi-access edge computing in 5G and beyond: fundamentals, technology integration, and state-of-the-art. IEEE Access **10**(8), 116974–7017 (2020)
2. ETSI. ETSI GS MEC 003 V3.1.1: Multi-access Edge Computing (MEC); Framework and Reference Architecture (2022). https://www.etsi.org/deliver/etsi_gs/MEC/001_099/003/03.01.01_60/gs_MEC003v030101p.pdf
3. ETSI.   MEC   Ecosystem.   https://mecwiki.etsi.org/index.php?title=MEC_Ecosystem. Accessed 4 Oct 2022

4. Blakley, J.R., Iyengar, R., Roy, M.: Simulating edge computing environments to optimize application experience. School of Computer Science Carnegie Mellon University, Technical report CMU-CS-20-135, November 2020

5. Gazda, R., Roy, M., Blakley, J., Sakr, A., Schuster, R.: Towards open and cross domain edge emulation - the AdvantEDGE platform. In: 2021 IEEE/ACM Symposium on Edge Computing (SEC), 14 December 2021, pp. 339–344. IEEE (2021)

6. Abdulmaksoud, M., Dehadrai, N., Castrillón, J., Sakr, A., Schuster, R.: Edge diagnostics platform: orchestration and diagnosis model for edge computing infrastructure. In: 2021 IEEE International Conference on Edge Computing (EDGE), 5 September 2021, pp. 51–59. IEEE (2011)

7. Burbano J, Sakr, A., Schuster, R.: Sliding-window approach for improving response time of mission-critical applications. In: 2020 IEEE 5th International Symposium on Smart and Wireless Systems within the Conferences on Intelligent Data Acquisition and Advanced Computing Systems (IDAACS-SWS), 17 September 2020, pp. 1–7. IEEE (2020)

8. Sakr, A., Mohiyadeen, S., Vruksharaj, B., Schuster, R.: QoS-aware score-based edge resource allocation model. In: 2020 IEEE 5th International Symposium on Smart and Wireless Systems within the Conferences on Intelligent Data Acquisition and Advanced Computing Systems (IDAACS-SWS), 17 September 2020, pp. 1–7. IEEE (2020)

9. Michel, R., Di Lallo, K., Robert, G.: AdvantEDGE: A Mobile Edge Emulation Platform (MEEP). GitHub. https://github.com/InterDigitalInc/AdvantEDGE. Accessed 4 Oct 2022

10. Kubernetes. https://kubernetes.io. Accessed 4 Oct 2022

11. Docker. https://www.docker.com. Accessed 4 Oct 2022

12. influxdata. InfluxDB https://www.influxdata.com. Accessed 4 Oct 2022

13. Google. Google Kubernetes Engine. https://cloud.google.com/kubernetes-engine. Accessed 4 Oct 2022

14. ETSI. ETSI GS MEC 021 V2.1.1: Multi-access Edge Computing (MEC); Application Mobility Service API (2020). https://www.etsi.org/deliver/etsi_gs/MEC/001_099/021/02.01.01_60/gs_MEC021v020101p.pdf

15. InterDigitalInc. AdvantEDGE. GitHub. https://interdigitalinc.github.io/AdvantEDGE/docs/overview/edge-services/ams/. Accessed 4 Oct 2022

16. Cruz, P., Achir, N., Viana, A.C.: On the edge of the deployment: a survey on multi-access edge computing. ACM Comput. Surv. (CSUR) **55**, 1–34 (2022)

17. Labriji, I., et al.: Mobility aware and dynamic migration of MEC services for the Internet of Vehicles. IEEE Trans. Netw. Serv. Manage. **18**(1), 570–84 (2021)

18. Kondo, T., Isawaki, K., Maeda, K.: Development and evaluation of the MEC platform supporting the edge instance mobility. In: 2018 IEEE 42nd Annual Computer Software and Applications Conference (COMPSAC), 23 July 2018, vol. 2, pp. 193–198. IEEE (2018)

19. Okwuibe, J., Haavisto, J., Harjula, E., Ahmad, I., Ylianttila, M.: Orchestrating service migration for low power MEC-enabled IoT devices. arXiv preprint, 30 May 2019. arXiv:1905.12959

20. Intel. Intel®Smart Edge Open. https://www.openness.org. Accessed 4 Oct 2022

21. Fondo-Ferreiro, P., et al.: Seamless multi-access edge computing application handover experiments. In: 2021 IEEE 22nd International Conference on High Performance Switching and Routing (HPSR), 7 June 2021, pp. 1–6. IEEE (2021)

22. Kaur, K., Guillemin, F., Sailhan, F.: Container placement and migration strategies for Cloud. A survey, fog and edge data centers (2022)

23. Schrettenbrunner, J.: Migrating Pods in Kubernetes (2020)
24. SSU-DCN. podmigration-operator. https://github.com/SSU-DCN/podmigration-operator/blob/main/init-cluster-containerd-CRIU.md. Accessed 4 Oct 2022
25. InterDigitalInc. AdvantEDGE. GitHub. https://github.com/InterDigitalInc/AdvantEDGE/tree/1e63a66e8820f0882c998f1cbc6d200bcd14f412. Accessed 4 Oct 2022
26. ETSI. ETSI GS MEC 013 V2.2.1: Multi-access Edge Computing (MEC); Location API (2022). https://www.etsi.org/deliver/etsi_gs/mec/001_099/013/02.01.01_60/gs_mec013v020101p.pdf
27. ETSI. ETSI GS MEC 012 V2.1.1: Multi-access Edge Computing (MEC); Radio Network Information API (2019). https://www.etsi.org/deliver/etsi_gs/MEC/001_099/012/02.01.01_60/gs_mec012v020101p.pdf
28. ETSI. ETSI GS MEC 028 V2.2.1: Multi-access Edge Computing (MEC); WLAN Access Information API. https://www.etsi.org/deliver/etsi_gs/MEC/001_099/028/02.02.01_60/gs_MEC028v020201p.pdf
29. ETSI. ETSI GS MEC 011 V2.2.1: Multi-access Edge Computing (MEC); Edge Platform Application Enablement. https://www.etsi.org/deliver/etsi_gs/MEC/001_099/011/02.02.01_60/gs_MEC011v020201p.pdf
30. Video LAN organization. Video LAN. https://www.videolan.org. Accessed 4 Oct 2022

Blockchain

An Efficient Data Retrieval Method
for Blockchain

Yafeng Li[1], Hang Huang[2], and Lichuan Ma[2(✉)]

[1] China CETC Key Laboratory of Technology on Data Link, Xi'an, China
xxddxdd@yeah.net
[2] Shaanxi Key Laboratory of Blockchain and Secure Computing, Xidian University,
Xi'an, China
lcma@xidian.edu.cn

Abstract. As blockchain has gained its popularity in different areas,
there would be an unimaginable amount of data to be tackled to support its much richer functionalities. As a result, an efficient data retrieval
method is of great significance for the development of blockchain. Thus,
in this paper, a novel and efficient data retrieval scheme that is compatible with the decentralized nature of blockchain is proposed. Specifically,
a new data structure for storing complex data is firstly put forward
to reduce the redundancy of data storage on the chain in distributed
storage scenario. Then, a counted bloom filter jump table structure that
integrating bloom filter and jump table structures is designed to improve
tag retrieval efficiency and enrich semantic queries in a low space occupation. Finally, extensive experiments have been conducted to verify the
performance of the proposed method in terms of the retrieval efficiency
and space ratio.

Keywords: blockchain · composite data · distributed storage ·
retrieval

1 Introduction

In recent years, the technology of blockchain has gained its popularity in different
areas. It can be seen that, in the future, blockchain will not only be a carrier of
decentralized cryptocurrency, but also a carrier of more and more applications.
As a result, there would be an unimaginable amount of data to be dealt with
blockchain to support its much richer functionalities.

Despite the increasing maturity of blockchain technology, most solutions
nowadays are for small data and large data on the chain. Like Ethereum and
Fabric, they take small data (referred as transactions) into considers. As for large
data, the works of VChain [1] and SEBDB [2] are proposed to tackle large files
more than 1G. All these methods work by the same way that data are stored
offchain and related credentials are stored onchain [3].

However, as blockchain becomes more prevalent in different fields, more and
more medium size of data, also named complex data, need to be dealt with

© ICST Institute for Computer Sciences, Social Informatics and Telecommunications Engineering 2023
Published by Springer Nature Switzerland AG 2023. All Rights Reserved
S. Yu et al. (Eds.): TridentCom 2022, LNICST 489, pp. 121–137, 2023.
https://doi.org/10.1007/978-3-031-33458-0_9

blockchain. Few solutions exist for tackling such kind of data. If existing methods are directly introduced, it will make the whole system less effective and efficient. Also, such systems are not able to be scaled to more complex applications. Similarly, distributed-storage-based blockchain systems encounter the same problem. This is because the data onchain are tamper-proof hash credentials for files and thus the retrieving process is prohibited. This results in the fact that a third party is still necessary for supporting retrieval.

Because of the simple structure of transactions in current blockchains, appending data to the chain is done in the form of full updates, where a considerable amount of data need to be repeatedly stored and lots of storage space are wasted. When extending to the scenario composite data storage, it is less desirable to append the latest data directly in the form of full volume updates because the system performance would be degraded seriously.

Also, existing well-designed retrieval schemes based on blockchain are not suitable for storing complex data. Moreover, an efficient retrieval method for composite data structures is still missing. If existing solutions are directly adopted here, the retrieval process goes from the lated block to the initial block one by one, which leads to ugly retrieval efficiency.

Thus in this paper, an efficient data retrieval method for blockchain is proposed to overcome the above limitations. The main contributions of this paper are:

1. A new data structure for storing complex data is put forward to reduce the redundancy of data storage on the chain in distributed storage scenario.
2. A counted bloom filter jump table structure that integrating bloom filter and jump table structures is designed to improve tag retrieval efficiency and enrich semantic queries in a low space occupation.
3. The proposed data retrieval scheme is practically implemented and its effectiveness and efficiency are verified via extensive experiments.

The rest of the paper is organized as follows. Related works are summarized in Sect. 2. In Sect. 3, the system model is present. Section 4 elaborates the proposed efficient data retrieval method. Comprehensive experimental results are demonstrated in Sect. 5 to verify the efficiency and effectiveness of the proposed method. At the end, Sect. 6 concludes this paper.

2   Related Works

Already in 2014, Wilkinson and Lowry released the distributed peer-to-peer cloud storage network blockchain Storj [4], which configures a trusted cloud storage system between a host and a client. All data must be encrypted before the client can transmit it to other users in the network. In addition, Storj uses atoshi-style metadata and stores it in an ethereum blockchain, which allows users to retrieve the full information they want when they need it.

Sia is another storage platform based on blockchain [5]. Sia's data storage nodes are referred to as hosts in this network. Also in the network there is a publicly available and verifiable proof of storage that contains a list of hashes in the file and a small portion of the original file data, so the user does not need to verify the file himself.

To enable blockchain to support the features of tamper-proofing, data version control, and fork semantics, Pingcheng Ruan et al. implemented Fork-Base [6], which not only achieves high performance but also reduces developer effort in developing programs by integrating core application properties into the store. LineageChain is also published in [7] to work as an efficient, secure and fine-grained blockchain system for data traceability. BlockchainDB is to utilize blockchain as the storage layer and introduce a database layer on top of the storage layer to participate in data sharing scenarios [8]. As this database layer uses a traditional database, it can be extended with data management techniques from traditional databases and a standardised query interface to facilitate the use of blockchain in data sharing scenarios. It also provides strong data consistency guarantees and an easy-to-use query interface, which improves the performance of blockchain retrieval systems and reduces the complexity of system complexity of use.

CAPER is proposed in [9], where they transformed the blockchain ledger from a chained structure to a directed acyclic graph. Here, each application only needs to maintain and access its own owned view of the ledger, which includes its all cross-application transactions and internal transactions. This solution provides an improvement in retrieval performance and thus increases the scalability of the blockchain. ChainSQL in [10] acts an application platform for blockchain databases developed by combining a database with a blockchain. ColChain in [11] divides the unstructured peer-to-peer network into smaller communities of nodes and applies data fragments in a community-based update chain. HyperQL's solution in [12] is to add a query layer on top of the Hyperledger Fabric, and a block listener is utilized to listen for blocks that have not been generated. With this approach, all the onchain data can be obtained. By this manner, the solution provides four advanced queries, namely basic queries, top k queries, range queries and extended queries. In [13], a new scheme for Ether history management based on directed acyclic graphs (DAGs) is put forward. The core idea of the scheme is to incorporate the concept of a DAG into a token design model. By doing this, various token histories, including merges, branches and splits, would be efficiently tracked. The authors of [14] propose the Ether Query Language (EQL), which allows users to retrieve information from the blockchain by writing SQL-like queries. This enables a wide variety of semantic queries and the problem of tracing historical data back to the initialization can be resolved to some extent.

However, existing blockchain systems do not fully satisfy all the requirements of distributed applications. The reason for this drawback is mainly due to the poor support for various data format. To solve this problem, a novel and efficient data retrieval scheme that is compatible with the decentralized nature of blockchain is proposed in this paper.

3   System Model

3.1   Overall Architecture

The proposed scheme for efficient retrieval of compound data in a distributed storage blockchain system is based on a multi-node decentralised network structure. Figure 1 below shows the overall architecture of the scheme, where the off-chain distributed storage network, p2p (peer to peer) nodes [15], and consensus mechanism are all existing technologies that provide the necessary environment for the composite data retrieval module in the scheme. The whole retrieval scheme is divided into two parts: the counting Bloom filter jumping table and the inter-block intra-block retrieval optimization. The counting Bloom filter jumping table is mainly designed to greatly improve the retrieval performance of the blockchain for compound data without taking up a large amount of storage space. The intra-block optimization changes the transaction structure to make it more suitable for storing compound data and speed up intra-block data retrieval; the inter-block optimization uses a directed acyclic graph to associate linked data on the chain together, eliminating the need to traverse the blockchain multiple times to retrieve it, we only need to find the latest data in the blockchain and use the topological sorting of points in the directed acyclic graph to get all the results quickly.

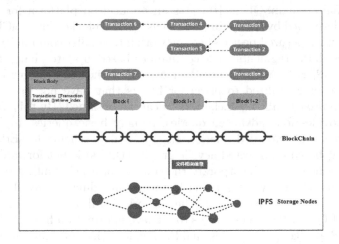

Fig. 1. Blockchain-based composite data retrieval architecture.

3.2   Problem Definition

We have a definition of composite data, which can only be called composite data if it satisfies the following characteristics: it can be split into smaller granular data; it can be stored at will; and when the data is needed, it can be combined according to a certain identical characteristic. In this scheme, the metadata obtained by splitting composite data is defined as

$$slice = <\delta, \tau, inf> \tag{1}$$

where, δ is referred as the key information, τ is the label, and inf stands for the corresponding piece from the splitted original data. In this paper, the retrieval of composite data is achieved by means of some data labels attached to it. From this sense, all the onchain data can be represented as a tuple $O_i = <\tau, v_i, inf>$, where v_i is the location on blockchain of the i-th metadata.

4   The Proposed Method

In the proposed method, there are two modules, the counting Bloom filter table-hopping scheme, and the inter- and intra-block retrieval optimization.

4.1   Counted Bloom Filter Jump Table Structure

In order to implement an efficient retrieval scheme, a counted Bloom filter jump table structure is put forward, which can be implemented by only one variable stored in the block header. There are two advantages: firstly, it implements a blockchain based scheme for efficient retrieval of data labels; secondly, only one Bloom filter variable of fixed length is used for each block, which greatly reduces storage space compared to other existing retrieval schemes.

Next, let's start with an overall implementation of the Counting Bloom Filter Jump Table structure, which is an innovative implementation of a blockchain similar to the Jump Table function using the feature that the blockchain can only append blocks backwards, and using a Counting Bloom Filter implemented by ourselves, which we call the Counting Bloom Filter Jump Table. The structure has the following characteristics.

The first point is that using a Bloom filter structure in each block can effectively improve the efficiency of queries. Specifically, the data in the blockchain is distributed in each block, and the amount of data contained in a single block is very small, so the user's query request is irrelevant to the content of most of the blocks, and the greatest value of the Bloom filter is that it can filter most of the useless requests. So by adding Bloom filters to the data tags that the user wants to retrieve in the blockchain, it will greatly speed up the retrieval efficiency.

The second point is that the counting Bloom filter structure used in this construction, which is an advanced version of the Bloom filter, allows Bloom filter to be used in the scenarios where precise detection results are required. For this particular scenario of blockchain composite data retrieval, it needs to use a counting Bloom filter to record the counts on each bit in each block, so that it is able to add or remove the Bloom filter values on blocks in certain intervals to achieve a similar function to jumping tables. While an unusual counting Bloom filter would require a variable to store the Bloom filter values and an array to record the number of occurrences of each value, we have combined the counters directly with the Bloom filter to better suit the low storage requirements.

This structure reduces the size of the stored data compared to a traditional counting Bloom filter, while the upper limit on the number of occurrences recorded per bit depends on the length of the entire Bloom filter; the longer the length, the larger the upper limit on the number of times each bit is recorded. The details for designing the counting Bloom filter are as following.

1. **Add method:** Since traditional Bloom filters require multiple hash functions to compute multiple hash values, it is too time consuming. Instead in this paper, a more efficient pseudo-random algorithm is used, which is a pseudo-random algorithm proposed in [16]. Although the maximum possible randomness cannot be achieved, for a blockchain where the data stored in each block is relatively small and there is a large amount of identical data, it is sufficient here to utilize a random distribution that is as even as possible.
2. **AddBloom and SubBloom methods:** These are two methods that process the current Bloom filter value, add or subtract the current Bloom filter value from other Bloom filter values, and reassign the result to the current Bloom filter value. Both of these methods are used to prepare for the implementation of the Counting Bloom Filter Jumping Table.
3. **Test method:** This method is used to check whether a particular piece of data exists in the current Bloom filter value and the output is Boolean, False means the data must not be stored in this Bloom filter value; True means the opposite result.

Before designing the solution, we have surveyed various traditional databases and cached database retrieval solutions and found that they all have a tree structure or jump table structure to assist the database to accelerate indexing. It would gain promising performance improvement when combining jump table and Bloom filter. The overall structure is shown in the following figure.

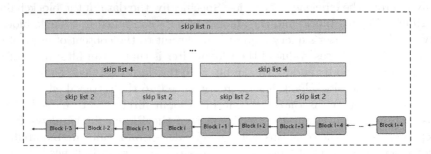

Fig. 2. Blockchain structure diagram for the jump table function.

Figure 2 means that skip List 2 stores the Bloom filter values in two adjacent blocks, which means that the Bloom filter at the head of Block i-2 stores not only the data in its own block body, but also stores the data in the previous block. Similarly, skip list n stores the Bloom filter values of the n neighbours, which means that Block n stores all the Bloom filter values from Block i-3 to

Block n. When a user initiates a query request, he first asks for the Bloom filter in the header of Block n. If it does not exist, then he can skip these n blocks and query again from Block i-2; if it does exist, then he needs to go through the blocks at the skip List $n - 1$ level to make further judgements.

The counting Bloom Filter Skip List (CBFS) structure derived from all of the above theoretical solutions is shown in Fig. 3.

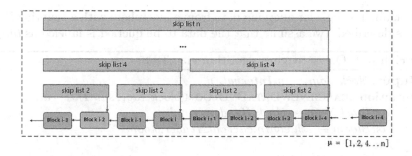

$$\mu = [1, 2, 4 \ldots n]$$

Fig. 3. Counting Bloom filter jump table structure.

Obviously, since we are implementing a counting Bloom filter jump table structure similar to the jump table function, a parameter $\mu = [i_0, i_1, i_2, \ldots, i_n]$ needs to be passed in, i.e. the interval and the number of layers of the CBFS, during the initialisation of the whole blockchain system. A brief description of the algorithm for the creation of counted Bloom filter values in new blocks is given.

Algorithm 1. CBFS value creation algorithm in a block.

1: **Input:** $O = < O_1, O_2, \ldots, O_n >$
2: Initialization a blank counted Bloom filter value: $newBloom$
3: $lastBlockNum \leftarrow eth.chain.currentHeader.Number$
4: **for** $i = 1, 2, \ldots, O.length$ **do**
5:     $newBloom.Add(O[i].\tau)$
6: **end for**
7: **for** $i = 1, 2, \ldots, \mu.length$ **do**
8:     $f \leftarrow \mu[i]$
9:     **if** $lastBlockNum\%f == 0$ **then**
10:         $start \leftarrow lastBlockNum - f + \mu[i - 1]$
11:         **for** $start < lastBlockNum$ **do**
12:             $b \leftarrow eth.getBlockByNumber(start).header.bloom$
13:             $newBloom.AddBloom(b)$
14:             $start \leftarrow \mu[i - 1]$
15:         **end for**
16:     **end if**
17: **end for**

---

1. Initialize a blank counting Bloom filter $newBloom$.
2. Store the labels to be retrieved in this block into the Counting Bloom Filter $newBloom$.
3. Calculate the current block at level i of the CBFS based on the latest block number $lastBlockNum$, and sum all the counted Bloom filters from the block $lastBlockNum - \mu[i]$ to the block $lastBlockNum - 1$ with $newBloom$ to obtain the Bloom filter value for the current block.

Then again, the logic for querying data from a blockchain with a counting Bloom filter is described: (we assume that the data to be queried is labeled as tag_1).

Algorithm 2. Query tagging algorithm via CBFS.

1: **Input:** $block$, tag_1, $sumInterval$, μ
2: **function** SEARCHNEWDATABYBLOOM($block, tag_1, sumInterval, \mu$)
3:    $lastBlockNum \leftarrow block.Header.Number$
4:    $lastBloom \leftarrow eth.chain.currentHeader.bloom$
5:    $Interval \leftarrow 1$
6:    $start \leftarrow lastBlockNum$
7:    $end \leftarrow lastBlockNum - sumInterval$
8:    **for** $start < end$ **do**
9:        **for** $i = \mu.length, \ldots, 1$ **do**
10:           **if** $blockNum\%\mu[i] == 0$ **then**
11:               $Interval \leftarrow \mu[i]$
12:               **if** $i == 0$ **then**
13:                   $eth.searchSingleData(tag_1, start)$
14:                   Initializing the stack space: $stack$
15:                   $j \leftarrow lastBlockNum - \mu[i - 1]$
16:                   **for** $j > lastBlockNum - \mu[i]$ **do**
17:                       $b \leftarrow eth.getBlockByNumber(j)$
18:                       **if** $b.bloom.Test(tag_1)$ **then**
19:                           $stack.push(b)$
20:                       **end if**
21:                       $block.SubBloom(b.bloom)$
22:                       $j \leftarrow j - \mu[i]$
23:                   **end for**
24:                   **for** $!stack.isEmpty()$ **do**
25:                       $b2 \leftarrow stack.pop()$
26:                       $searchNewDataByBloom(b2, tag_1, \mu[i], \mu[: i])$
27:                   **end for**
28:               **end if**
29:           **end if**
30:        **end for**
31:        $start \leftarrow start - interval$
32:    **end for**
33: **end function**

---

1. First get the latest block number *blockNum* and the Bloom filter value *block.bloom* stored in its block header, and use the block number to determine the number of jump table i where this block is in.
2. Start with the block of $blockNum - \mu_i$, and if the block number is not at the bottom of the counting Bloom filter, recursively repeat the first step so that $blockNum \leftarrow blockNum - \mu_i$.
3. The Bloom filter of the block blockNum-mui determines whether this data may exist in the current block and, if so, puts the block on a temporary stack. The Bloom filter of this block is also subtracted from block.bloom. Then loop the third step towards the block with $blockNum - \mu_i + \mu_{i-1}$ until this block equals *blockNum*.
4. The subtracted *block.bloom* is used to determine if the data may exist in the current block, and if so, it is placed on a temporary stack.
5. From the temporary stack, one by one, the block will come out of the stack, so as to determine whether the data of tag_1 exists in this block, if not, then loop the next one until it is found, and return the corresponding data.

Of course, a simple counted Bloom filter jump table would suffer from performance degradation when the number of blocks increases due to its small footprint. To compensate for this, as well as for better storage of composite data and faster retrieval performance, our solution also makes certain optimizations between and within blocks of the blockchain.

4.2 Inter- and Intra-block Search Performance Optimization

Firstly, the optimization method within the block is introduced. For the existing transaction structures in public chain (i.e. Bitcoin and Ethereum), most of them are designed to be applied in cryptocurrency scenarios. Here, the data structure of transmission storage is very simple. This leads to that the current transaction structure is also very simple. However, in non-transaction scenarios where the blockchain technology is adopted, this simple transaction structure is not very reasonable. In order to be able to enrich the retrieval semantics as well as to speed up the retrieval process, the structure of transaction is redesigned in this paper to make it more suitable for non-transactional scenarios. This new block body structure is as follows (Tables 1, 2 and 3).

Table 1. Structure block body information.

Field	Type	Comment
Transactions	[ ]*Transaction	Storage transactions
Retrieve	[ ]Retrieve_index	Composite data index area

Table 2. Structure Retrieve_index Information.

Field	Type	Comment
Tag	String	Data labels
OrderArray	[ ][ ]int	Information on the location of composite data storage
PreviousBlockIndex	int	Location index of the previous block

Table 3. Structure Transaction information.

Field	Type	Comment
TxID	Int	Transaction ID
Time	Time	Transaction initiation time
Data	[ ]StorageData	Composite data information

Inspired by the idea of inverted indexing from traditional search engines, the block is divided into two parts, a data retrieval area and a data storage area. Similar to inverted indexing, the data retrieval area is constructed by tagging the data in the current block.

Recall that composite data stored on the blockchain can be split into smaller granularity and be reconstructed whenever it is needed. The modified block body here is very suitable for storing such kind of data. The *Data* structure in transactions contains the information related to the original composite data, as well as the data content itself. Whenever needed, the original composite data can be reconstructed by gathering all the *Data*s on blockchain. When some *Data*s related to the composite data need to be modified, it is not necessary to upload the whole data to the blockchain but only the changed ones need to be uploaded.

The process for storing composite data are as follows.

1. Data processing under the chain, splitting the composite data into $slice = <\delta, \tau, inf>$.
2. The user uploads the data *slice* to the blockchain via the node.
3. Parsing the data, storing the resultant data in the *Data* structure of the transaction and recording its position in the block body, storing the position information τ with the Retrieve_index structure for subsequent queries.

The process of modifying the composite data is a little simpler. Firstly, the metadata of the composite data to be modified is retrieved. Then, the information inf in this metadata is modified. Finally, the modified information is uploaded to the blockchain to complete the modification process. Since δ and τ in the slice are unchanged, these two pieces of information can be used to locate all the latest metadata when retrieving it and return all the query results to the user. By doing this, the user can restore and combine the latest composite data.

As for the inter-block optimization, a directed acyclic graph-based design is utilized. The core idea of doing this is to associate linked data on the chain with each other and return the final query result without having to traverse the entire block chain to complete the retrival.

If a new tag appears in a transaction, we assign an initial tag number to that tag. When encountering a continuation of an existing tag, an existing tag number plusing one is assigned to that tag. If more than one transaction exists in a block, the transaction in that block is considered to be an extension of some previous state in the block database. In this case, the latest tag number of a data tag in the system is simultaneously added with the block number. From a macroscopic point of view, a directed acyclic graph is constructed from these different labels and the corresponding label relationships. At this point, we just need to find the latest label number and use the point topology sorting in the directed acyclic graph to get all the results quickly.

The above structure is implemented by adding an index to each tag in the Retrieve_index area of the block body and a version field to each data in the Storage Data area. The latest data tag is queried by a counted Bloom filter jumping the table structure, then the index is used to find the last block in which the tag was stored, and so on until the value is empty. This eliminates the need to use the Counting Bloom filter multiple times during the blockchain retrieval process and greatly enhances retrieval performance.

In addition, we have designed our own novel Merkle DAG structure based on the above DAG in order to facilitate user verifications of the query results' correctness. The process of building this structure is roughly as follows: a hash value is calculated for the search area; then, a hash value for each transaction is obtained; a Merkle tree is derived via all these hash values and the root node is stored in the block header.

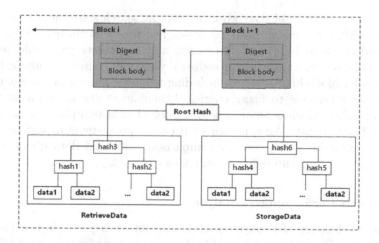

Fig. 4. Directed acyclic graph structure.

From Fig. 4, the verifiable identity structure is also a Merkle hash tree. Differently, the root hash of this tree is made by hashing both the root hash of the Merkle hash tree of the retrieved data area and the root hash of the Merkle hash tree of the stored data area. When the user gets their query results, the path hashes are also obtained. The user can then work out the root hash from these hashes, and the correctness of the data can then be verified in an easy way.

Moreover, it is also possible to verify the integrity of the data by using the Merkle DAG tree to ensure that the data obtained are genuine and trustworthy.

5 Experiments

In this section, a prototype of the proposed method is implemented. It consists of counted Bloom filter jump tables, intra-block index optimization and inter-block index optimization. The counted Bloom filter jump table is responsible for providing a structure with low storage space and high retrieval efficiency; the intra-block index optimization is responsible for optimising the storage of compound data, supporting multiple query methods and incremental update structures. The inter-block index optimization is responsible for reducing the number of retrievals and retrieval time.

Our experimental evaluation is used to test the following three aspects.

1. **Search performance.** The main purpose is to simulate and test the relationship between the volume of data on the blockchain and the response time of various retrieval methods.
2. **Storage performance.** The main objective is to test how the storage space occupied by the whole blockchain system changes as the amount of data on the blockchain increases, to see if our solution has a strong competitive advantage.

The most recent published work on efficient search solutions for blockchain systems is MST [2], which both addresses real-time distributed search for on-chain and off-chain hybrid architectures, and constructs to enable real-time search of blockchain data while providing a variety of complex analytical search primitives for blockchain systems, including semantic queries and range queries, while being extensible to fuzzy queries. Ethereum is one of the most mature platforms today, which is an open source public blockchain platform with smart contract functionality. We compare with these two systems in various aspects such as transaction query latency comparison, historical data query, multiple data tagging, system throughput and space footprint.

5.1 Search Performance Analysis

The search efficiency of the system is divided into two parts. In this thesis, we use a counting Bloom filter jump table structure to improve the search efficiency, compared to the traditional blockchain search method, which needs to traverse the data on the whole blockchain from the latest block until the creation block stops, and as the number of blocks keeps growing, the search time will become unacceptable. In contrast to the original blockchain search method, our solution uses an index structure to search the data on the chain and achieves a time complexity of $O(logN)$ without intra-block and inter-block optimization, where N is the number of blocks multiplied by the number of transactions, and as the number of blocks grows, the efficiency advantage of our solution becomes more and more obvious.

History Data Query Performance. When comparing data queries, in addition to using our own solution and traditional ethereum, we also compare the MST solution, which creates an MST tree structure that also optimises the speed of retrieval of past data queries in the blockchain. In this experiment, we directly test the performance of traditional ethereum by calling the underlying interface implementation, as smart contracts do not currently support retrieval of history data over time.

Two separate sets of experiments were conducted to demonstrate the performance of each solution for retrieving history data in various ways.

In the first group, we first use the code to post update transactions so that more than 10,000 blocks are stored in the blockchain ledger. Then perform queries on the data in different history intervals to see the respective performance. The experiment evaluates the impact of each scenario on query latency as the distance to the last block increased.

Figure 5 illustrates the increase in query latency as the distance to the last block increases. It can be seen that the traditional Ethernet retrieval scheme has the lowest latency when the distance is small. Traditional Ethernet does not build complex retrieval indexes, so for such queries it requires a linear scan from the latest version. Therefore, when the requested version is very new, it will be fast because the number of reads is small. However, as the distance increases, its performance degrades rapidly.

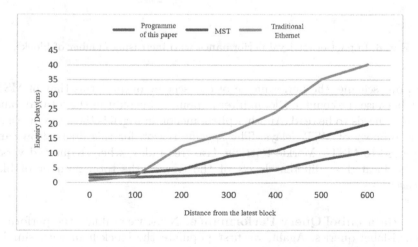

Fig. 5. Effect of search performance with distance.

It can also be observed that the latency in the query MST scheme is lower than in the traditional Ethernet scheme. This is because the query uses the Merkle Patricia Trie index directly. Our blockchain-based composite data retrieval scheme outperforms the other two solutions. This is because in our scheme, not only do we use counted Bloom filters and jump tables to speed up the retrieval, but also use DAGs for inter-block topological indexing, and intra-block indexing optimization. By this manner, the latency in our scheme is very low when the block distance increases, rather than increasing linearly towards the traditional Ethernet retrieval scheme.

In the second group, the first experiment is repeated, but this time with a fixed number of block intervals, and the effect of each scenario on the query latency as the number of blocks in the blockchain increases. This time, the experiment was conducted with a fixed number of block intervals of 100 and gradually increasing the number of blocks in the blockchain, and the query latency of each solution was analysed for the current case.

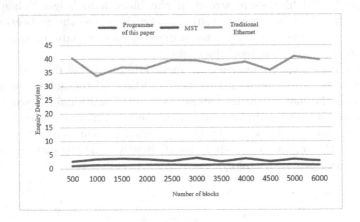

Fig. 6. Impact of retrieval performance with increasing number of blocks.

In our scheme, the performance of our scheme outperforms that of MST in Fig. 6 because the counted Bloom filter hopping table reduces the total amount of data that needs to be read. Another phenomenon in Fig. 6 is the large fluctuation in the number of MST delays. The specific reason for this fluctuation can be attributed to MST's Merkle Patricia Trie tree index, where requested versions may be located at different levels of the tree as the total number of blocks increases.

Multi-data Label Query Performance. Next, we evaluate the performance of multi-label queries. Again, we first populate the blockchain with simulated data, and then we publish a transaction querying multi-label data to analyse the multi-label query performance of each scenario. In this experiment, we compare different search depths to analyse performance.

In this experiment, we compare the latency for multiple data label queries in six blockchains of different depths.

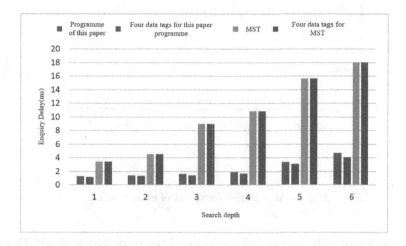

Fig. 7. The impact of multi-tag searching on search performance.

Figure 7 shows the effect of single-tag retrieval as well as four-tag retrieval on retrieval performance, and we can see that the overall retrieval performance of our scheme is better than that of the MST scheme. Also, comparing the effect of different number of tags on retrieval performance for the same scheme, it can be seen from the figure that the retrieval performance for multi-tag retrieval is equivalent to that of single-tag indexing due to the Merkle Patricia Trie tree indexing of MST. Our solution, on the other hand, is optimised for multi-label retrieval, with the higher the number of labels, the shorter the response time for retrieval.

5.2 Storage Performance Analysis

The counted Bloom filter jump table in our solution only requires one Bloom value to be added to each block header, while our inter- and intra-block optimization does not add too much field information. Since existing blockchain-based personalised retrieval solutions, however, mostly come at the cost of taking up a lot of system hard disk space, the space footprint of our solution is much smaller than other existing solutions for data tag retrieval on blockchains.

In order to test the overall space occupation performance of the scheme, by comparing the space occupation of their own scheme with the MHT scheme and the two traditional Ethernet schemes, all three projects were tested for the storage of data, by using the same data set, tens of thousands of data writes were performed, and the overall storage space occupation of the blockchain was tested for four nodes with different amounts of data, the test results are shown in the following figure.

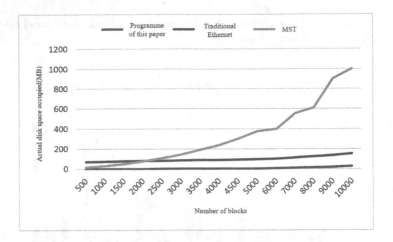

Fig. 8. Actual disk footprint of each solution.

Figure 8 shows the actual disk footprint of the respective schemes. Our solution outperforms the MST solution as well as the traditional ethereum smart contract solution. The reason for this is that our solution only adds a Bloom filter variable to each block header, and also makes certain optimizations to the storage of compound data in the block body, enabling incremental data update operations, further reducing the data disk footprint of the blockchain. The Merkle Patricia Trie tree index built in the MST, on the other hand, increases dramatically as the data increases. The traditional ethereum smart contract solution does not conform to the data structure of the composite data store, so when the data is updated, it needs to be updated in full, and cannot be updated incrementally as in this paper.

6   Conclusion

In this paper, a novel and efficient data retrieval scheme that is compatible with the decentralized nature of blockchain is proposed. Firstly, a new data structure for storing complex data is put forward to reduce the redundancy of data storage on the chain in distributed storage scenario. Then, a counted bloom filter jump table structure that integrating bloom filter and jump table structures is designed to improve tag retrieval efficiency and enrich semantic queries in a low space occupation. Finally, extensive experiments have been conducted to verify the performance of the proposed method in terms of the retrieval efficiency and space ratio.

Acknowledgement. This work is supported by the National Key Research and Development Program of China under Grant 2021YFB2700600, the National Natural Science Foundation of China under Grant 62132013 and 61902292, the Key Research and Development Programs of Shaanxi under Grants 2021ZDLGY06-03.

References

1. Xu, C., Zhang, C., Xu, J.: vChain: enabling verifiable Boolean range queries over blockchain databases. In Proceedings of the 2019 International Conference on Management of Data, pp. 141–158, June 2019
2. Pei, Q., Zhou, E., Xiao, Y., Zhang, D., Zhao, D.: An efficient query scheme for hybrid storage blockchains based on Merkle Semantic Trie. In: 2020 International Symposium on Reliable Distributed Systems (SRDS), pp. 51–60. IEEE, September 2020
3. Eberhardt, J., Heiss, J.: Off-chaining models and approaches to off-chain computations. In: Proceedings of the 2nd Workshop on Scalable and Resilient Infrastructures for Distributed Ledgers, pp. 7–12, December 2018
4. Wilkinson, S., Lowry, J., Boshevski, T.: Metadisk a blockchain-based decentralized file storage application. Storj Labs Inc., Technical report, hal, 1–11 (2014)
5. Vorick, D., Champine, L.: Sia: simple decentralized storage (2018). Accessed 8 May 2014
6. Wang, S., et al.: ForkBase: an efficient storage engine for blockchain and forkable applications. arXiv preprint arXiv:1802.04949 (2018)
7. Ruan, P., Chen, G., Dinh, T.T.A., Lin, Q., Ooi, B.C., Zhang, M.: Fine-grained, secure and efficient data provenance on blockchain systems. Proc. VLDB End. **12**(9), 975–988 (2019)
8. El-Hindi, M., Binnig, C., Arasu, A., Kossmann, D., Ramamurthy, R.: BlockchainDB: a shared database on blockchains. Proc. VLDB Endow. **12**(11), 1597–1609 (2019)
9. Amiri, M.J., Agrawal, D., Abbadi, A.E.: CAPER: a cross-application permissioned blockchain. Proc. VLDB Endow. **12**(11), 1385–1398 (2019)
10. Muzammal, M., Qu, Q., Nasrulin, B., Skovsgaard, A.: A blockchain database application platform. arXiv preprint arXiv:1808.05199 (2018)
11. Aebeloe, C., Montoya, G., Hose, K.: ColChain: collaborative linked data networks. In: Proceedings of the Web Conference 2021, pp. 1385–1396, April 2021
12. Lin, Y.J., Sun, M.T.: HyperQL-efficient blockchain query. In: TANET 2018 Taiwan Internet Conference, pp. 939–944 (2018)
13. Watanabe, H., et al.: Enhancing blockchain traceability with DAG-based tokens. In: 2019 IEEE International Conference on Blockchain (Blockchain), pp. 220–227. IEEE, July 2019
14. Bragagnolo, S., Rocha, H., Denker, M., Ducasse, S.: Ethereum query language. In: Proceedings of the 1st International Workshop on Emerging Trends in Software Engineering for Blockchain, pp. 1–8, May 2018
15. Schollmeier, R.: A definition of peer-to-peer networking for the classification of peer-to-peer architectures and applications. In: Proceedings of the First International Conference on Peer-to-Peer Computing, pp. 101–102. IEEE, August 2001
16. Aumasson, J.-P., Bernstein, D.J.: SipHash: a fast short-input PRF. In: Galbraith, S., Nandi, M. (eds.) INDOCRYPT 2012. LNCS, vol. 7668, pp. 489–508. Springer, Heidelberg (2012). https://doi.org/10.1007/978-3-642-34931-7_28

Machine learning

A Survey on 3D Style Transfer

Qifeng Zhu[✉], Min Sun, and Jiang Wang

Suzhou City University, Suzhou, China
qifeng_zhu@szcu.edu.cn

Abstract. Image style transfer is a popular and widely studied task in computer vision, and it aims to apply the style of the source image to the target while the target remains its original content. Style transfer is widely used in creating new images in 2D, but style transfer in 3D images still has many challenges. In this paper, we summarize the major existing methods of 3D style transfer, including traditional and neural network based approaches. Moreover, we discuss the application field and the future research direction in 3D style transfer.

Keywords: 3D Images · Style Transfer · Neural Networks

1 Introduction

Style transfer is widely researched by many researchers. The traditional way to make an image style transfer is by picking up the texture information of a sample, then applying the texture to the target image. In 2001, Efros et al. [1] created a style transfer image using a quilting and texture synthesis algorithm. Although it works well on texture transfer, it has a limitation in extracting the deep feature information and realizing the style transfer in a more complex situation. With the development of machine learning, Gatys et al. [2] proposed an original idea of style transfer based on Convolutional Neural Networks. Since then, picking up feature maps by using convolutional networks to realize the 2D image style transfer has been expanded upon. However, there are few studies on 3D style transformation because the 3D graphics structure is complex, it contains spatial information. Style transfer methods in the 2D field cannot be directly used for 3D style transfer, and further changes and optimization are needed. This paper introduces the 3D style transfer method in both traditional ways and based on machine learning. We discuss the advantages and limitations of each method and the applications in the 3D style transfer field.

2 3D Style Transfer

2.1 Non-neural Network 3D Style Transfer

Before Gatys proposed [2], the traditional way to make 3D style transfer was through non-neural networks. For instance, Zheng et al. [3] make style transfer by decomposing the 3D model into parts, then restructuring them with similar visual structures. In contrast,

© ICST Institute for Computer Sciences, Social Informatics and Telecommunications Engineering 2023
Published by Springer Nature Switzerland AG 2023. All Rights Reserved
S. Yu et al. (Eds.): TridentCom 2022, LNICST 489, pp. 141–148, 2023.
https://doi.org/10.1007/978-3-031-33458-0_10

Ribeiro et al. [4] resemble the individual parts based on style features. Ma et al. proposed an analogy-driven 3D style transfer [5] to apply the style feature of an example to the target in the 3D field. This method is inspired by cognitive science; it works well in creating 3D models for geometric shapes. The framework of the method is illustrated in Fig. 1.

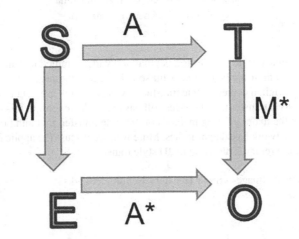

Fig. 1. Analogy relationships [5]

S, T, and E represent the source, target, and example input sets. O is the model of our goal. M is the result of computing the exemplar-source correspondence, and A is the result of computing the source-to-target transformations [5]. In the certain shape analogy quiz setup, M* is similar to M; according to this approximate A* by MAM^{-1}. This method can capture style features in fine-level, such as geometric textures or shapes, but it is limited to shapes with clearly separable [5].

2.2 3D Style Transfer Through Machine Learning

With the development of machine learning, researchers try to get a better style transfer result through neural networks. There are two different directions in neural network 3D style transfer. One is the "Decompose-assemble model" which has two steps: transform the 3D model into 2D images and then recreate the 3D model by processing style-transferred 2D images. The other is directly making a 3D style transfer through a 3D neural network without the deconstruction and reconstruction.

Decompose-assemble Model. Cutting the 3D model into plans or capturing the 2D pixel information of corresponding angles by surrounding the 3D model is an effective way of translating the 3D model to 2D images [6]. The style transfer process based on image iteration is proposed by Gatys, captures feature map information through VGG(Visual Geometry Group Network), creates Gram matrix as style feature from feature map of content and style image, computes the content loss and style loss, and optimizes the loss through gradient descent method. Formula (1) express the total loss faction in [2]; α and β are the weighting parameters for content and style reconstruction [2].

$$J(G) = \alpha J_{content}(C, G) + \beta J_{style}(S, G) \tag{1}$$

Although the image iteration-based style transfer has an excellent visual effect, the optimization is through back propagation, which is slow and costly. Since the adversarial generative network is created by Goodfellow [7], it is also used in the style transfer field. Especially, Zhu et al. proposed an unsupervised adversarial generative network, CycleGAN, which has two pairs of generators and discriminators [8]. The CycleGAN realizes bidirectional domain conversion to transfer style between unpaired examples. The final step is the reconstruction 3D model from style-transferred 2D images. There are multiple ways to reassemble the 3Dmodel, one of the ways Ren used in [9] is to get grayscale value from stylized images, then relocate the pixelized points to the original level in the spire volume according to the grayscale value, apply the smooth algorithm for final form modification [9].

Towards 3DNet. Different from 2D image data, which is usually represented as pixels, the representations of 3D images shape are point clouds, meshes, et; as a result, users, to make a style transfer through a 3D neural network directly, need to choose or create a 3DNet first. Timo [10] summarized common shape representations of 3D style transfer, which correspond to different 3DNet, including voxel, point cloud, surface mesh, and octree graph. Voxels are the straightforward extension of 2D pixels [10]; the detail information relates to the resolution size of voxels, which is less efficient than surface mesh and octree graph [10], while a point cloud is a simple list of 3D points in space. Jo [11] utilized PointNet [12] for realize 3D style transfer directly. However, different from the original style transfer system, he chooses the Hausdorff distance and the Chamfer distance as metrics to consider for loss functions, $d(x, y)$ which is the Euclidean distance [11].

$$d_H(X, Y) = \max\left\{\max_{x\in X}\min_{y\in Y}d(x, y), \max_{y\in Y}\min_{x\in X}d(x, y)\right\} \tag{2}$$

$$d_C(X, Y) = \sum_{x\in X}\min_{y\in Y}d(x, y) + \sum_{y\in Y}\min_{x\in X}d(x, y) \tag{3}$$

In addition, 3DNet style transfer based on Gram Matrix is also effective; however, the regular Gram Matrix in 3DNet style transfer has noisy results. To improve the result, Timo proposed standardization of Gram Matrix. According to the experiment, the style loss value is smaller for the small cube than for the sphere to avoid size changing by using the corresponding activation map [13].

$$G_{ij,s}^l = \frac{G_{ij}^l - \mu(G_{ij}^l)}{\sigma(G_{ij}^l)} \tag{4}$$

$$E_{l,s} = \sum_{(i,j)}\left(G_{ij,s}^l - A_{ij,s}^l\right)^2 \tag{5}$$

Here, μ and σ denote the mean and standard variation of a given tensor [14].

Either style transfer based on voxel-Gram Matrix or PointNet depends on generating labels to supervise, Mattia et al. proposed an unsupervised 3DNet style transfer model [15], which addresses by learning style-dependent generative models and adopt AtlasNet [16] and MeshFlow [17] decoders to generate style-dependent output distributions [15].

3   Application of 3D Style Transfer

3.1   Medical Data

For a long time, machine learning based on 2D images has been a powerful tool for diagnosing or evaluating diseases. Compared to the 2D model, 3D has a better visual effect to help doctors judge the lesion.

Therefore, a large 3D medical image data set is essential. Traditional 3D medical images can be obtained from thick 3D planes sampled from manually labeled anisotropic volumetric scans [18, 19]. However, we can now use 3D style transfer to obtain multi-modal 3D medical image datasets. For instance, Cesare Magnetti et al. slice each XCAT volume along the z-axis and retain style from a collection of 15 unique CT images per volume, and content from a window of ± 3 slices along the z-axis [20], to obtain abundant 4-Chamber 3D view datasets.

3.2   Virtual and Augmented Reality

With the development of augmented reality, 3D style conversion is also applied in augmented reality. Like the popular augmented reality game Pokémon GO, people can enrich more pets and increase play ability through 3D style transfer. Also, in virtual reality development, 3D scenes make people immersive, and furniture styles based on 3D style transfer are diversified, which is convenient for interior designers to create and design. Moreover, 3D style transfer could also be used to create human body shapes and help users customize the character images of the virtual world [21], thereby enhancing the social presence in virtual games and collaborative environments [15].

3.3   Animation Modeling

Animation modeling is perhaps the most prominent among the many application domains that 3D style transfer targets. With the rapid development of 3D animation and the game industry, there is a huge demand for 3D scene modeling. In particular, rich architectural scenes are usually large-scale and rich in details, and manual rendering modeling takes a long time. The 3D style conversion can change the shape of the building and change the texture details of the surface. Various combinations can produce multiple architectural styles, significantly reducing the workload of animation modeling. With the rise of the meta-universe, the establishment of a large number of character models can rely on 3D style conversion technology to achieve rapid and effective changes. For instance, Joao et al. [22] realized that 3D Human Shape Style Transfer includes skeletal motion and shape motion through the Generative Adversarial Network.

4   Future Research Direction of 3D Style Transfer

4.1   Algorithm and Parameter Optimization

In order to obtain stylized and ideal image results, it is necessary to manually adjust the parameters, especially based on the model optimization method. After each adjustment of the model parameters, the model needs to be retrained. Moreover, the model of a neural network can be optimized; Timo proposed normalization standardization to improve the result with less noise and optimized the activate function with elu(x) to enhance the neural work quality. Therefore, algorithm and parameter optimization is of great significance to the further development of image 3D style transfer.

4.2   Model Optimization

In contrast to 2D images, where color and texture are the dominant artistic style features, the representations of 3D images are point clouds and meshes. Therefore, the directly 3d style transfer changes the shape of the original 3D model but lacks texture detail information. Currently, the 3D style transformation needs two networks to realize the transformation of texture and shape, respectively. The final results are superimposed together. Finding new 3D data patterns or optimizing existing models, creating new 3D neural networks, which can transform the structure and surface details of 3D models at the same time, is also a research direction for future exploration.

4.3   Algorithm Evaluation

As a derivative of artistic creation, 3D style transfer is usually difficult to have an objective evaluation standard. Some researchers have invited volunteers to score the images after the style change. This method has two disadvantages. One is that there are not enough volunteers and the sample size is not large enough to be representative. On the other hand, the results are affected by personal preferences and a lack of persuasiveness and objectivity. Mattia et al. proposed 3D-LPIPS and STS, two new metrics used to measure 3D perceptual similarity and style transfer effectiveness [15], which is instructive to the objective quantitative analysis of 3D style transformation. A standard evaluation method is helpful in understanding how to improve the existing style transfer algorithm in the 3D field.

5   Discussion

3D style transfer has been a new research field of image migration in recent years. Especially compared with traditional methods, 3D style transfer based on neural networks has more flexibility and style diversity. Among the above studies, we summarized the advantages and limitations of each method as well as the major loss functions used in 3D style transfer (Tables 1 and 2).

Table 1. The advantages and disadvantages of the method we summarized to use in the 3D style transfer field.

Method	Advantages	Disadvantages
Based on analogy-driven [5]	Capture fine-level style features.	Constrained by rigid similarity transformation [5].
Decompose-assemble model	Well done in the texture transfer of the 3D model.	Lack of structure transfer.
Supervised 3DNet style transfer model	Well done in the structure transfer of the 3D model.	A large number of Labels need to be generated.
Unsupervised 3DNet style transfer model	Based on classification, there is no need to generate a large number of labels.	Classification could be attribute to errors, thus affecting the final result.

Table 2. An overview of major loss functions used in the 3D style transfer field.

Paper	Loss	Description
Gatys et al. [2]	Gram Loss [2]	The style loss based on Gram-based style representations is also useful in the 3D field [23].
Jo et al.[11]	Hausdorff and Chamfer Loss [11]	Reflect the similarity of 3D shapes.
Li and Wand [24]	Adversarial Loss [24]	More efficient retention of coherent textures in complex images compared to Gram Loss [23].

6 Conclusions

The methods of 3D style transfer are comprehensively described, including traditional image segmentation, fusion, and convolutional neural networks. In this paper, the current application fields of 3D style transfer are analyzed and summarized, as well as possible research hotspots in the future. Image style transfer based on deep learning is a hot research field with rapid development. This paper classifies and describes the current research work according to the main principles of image style transfer, which can help beginners and researchers in this field grasp the current research direction and deepen their understanding of the research.

Acknowledgment. This work was supported partly by the 2021 National pre-research project of Suzhou City University (2021SGY010).

References

1. Efros, A.A., Freeman, W.T.: Image quilting for texture synthesis and transfer. In: Proceedings of the 28th annual conference on Computer graphics and interactive techniques, pp. 341-346. (2001)
2. Gatys, L.A., Ecker, A.S., Bethge, M.: A neural algorithm of artistic style. arXiv preprint arXiv:1508.06576 (2015)
3. Zheng, Y., Cohen-Or, D., Mitra, N.J.: Smart variations: Functional substructures for part compatibility. In: Computer Graphics Forum, pp. 195-204. Wiley Online Library, (2013)
4. Ribeiro, P., Pereira, F.C., Marques, B.F., Leitão, B., Cardoso, A., Polo, I., de Marrocos, P.: A Model for Creativity in Creature Generation. In: GAME-ON, pp. 19–21. (2003)
5. Ma, C., Huang, H., Sheffer, A., Kalogerakis, E., Wang, R.: Analogy-driven 3D style transfer. In: Computer Graphics Forum, pp. 175–184. Wiley Online Library, (2014)
6. Zhang, H., Blasetti, E.: 3D architectural form style transfer through machine learning. In: Proceedings of the 25th International Conference of the Association for Computer-Aided Architectural Design Research in Asia (CAADRIA), pp. 659–668. (2020)
7. Goodfellow, I., Pouget-Abadie, J., Mirza, M., Xu, B., Warde-Farley, D., Ozair, S., Courville, A., Bengio, Y.: Generative adversarial nets. Advances in neural information processing systems 27, (2014)
8. Zhu, J.-Y., Park, T., Isola, P., Efros, A.A.: Unpaired image-to-image translation using cycle-consistent adversarial networks. In: Proceedings of the IEEE international conference on computer vision, pp. 2223–2232. (2017)
9. Ren, Y., Zheng, H.: Voxel-based 3D Neural Style Transfer. In: Proceedings of the 25th International Conference of the Association for Computer-Aided Architectural Design Research in Asia (CAADRIA), pp. 619–628. (2020)
10. Friedrich, T., Aulig, N., Menzel, S.: On the potential and challenges of neural style transfer for three-dimensional shape data. In: Rodrigues, H.C., et al. (eds.) EngOpt 2018, pp. 581–592. Springer, Cham (2019). https://doi.org/10.1007/978-3-319-97773-7_52
11. Mazeika, J., Whitehead, J.: Towards 3D Neural Style Transfer. In: AIIDE Workshops. (2018)
12. Qi, C.R., Su, H., Mo, K., Guibas, L.J.: Pointnet: Deep learning on point sets for 3d classification and segmentation. In: Proceedings of the IEEE conference on computer vision and pattern recognition, pp. 652–660. (2017)
13. Friedrich, T., Menzel, S.: Standardization of gram matrix for improved 3D neural style transfer. In: 2019 IEEE Symposium Series on Computational Intelligence (SSCI), pp. 1375–1382. IEEE, (2019)
14. Friedrich, T., Wollstadt, P., Menzel, S.: The effects of non-linear operators in voxel-based deep neural networks for 3D style reconstruction. In: 2020 IEEE Symposium Series on Computational Intelligence (SSCI), pp. 1460–1468. IEEE, (2020)
15. Segu, M., Grinvald, M., Siegwart, R., Tombari, F.: 3dsnet: Unsupervised shape-to-shape 3d style transfer. arXiv preprint arXiv:2011.13388 (2020)
16. Groueix, T., Fisher, M., Kim, V.G., Russell, B.C., Aubry, M.: A papier-mâché approach to learning 3d surface generation. In: Proceedings of the IEEE conference on computer vision and pattern recognition, pp. 216–224. (2018)
17. Gupta, K.: Neural mesh flow: 3d manifold mesh generation via diffeomorphic flows. University of California, San Diego (2020)
18. Alansary, A., et al.: Automatic view planning with multi-scale deep reinforcement learning agents. In: Frangi, A.F., Schnabel, J.A., Davatzikos, C., Alberola-López, C., Fichtinger, G. (eds.) MICCAI 2018. LNCS, vol. 11070, pp. 277–285. Springer, Cham (2018). https://doi.org/10.1007/978-3-030-00928-1_32

19. Lu, X., et al.: Automatic view planning for cardiac MRI acquisition. In: Fichtinger, G., Martel, A., Peters, T. (eds.) MICCAI 2011. LNCS, vol. 6893, pp. 479–486. Springer, Heidelberg (2011). https://doi.org/10.1007/978-3-642-23626-6_59

20. Magnetti, C., Reynaud, H., Kainz, B.: Cross Modality 3D Navigation Using Reinforcement Learning and Neural Style Transfer. arXiv preprint arXiv:2111.03485 (2021)

21. Yifan, W., Aigerman, N., Kim, V.G., Chaudhuri, S., Sorkine-Hornung, O.: Neural cages for detail-preserving 3d deformations. In: Proceedings of the IEEE/CVF Conference on Computer Vision and Pattern Recognition, pp. 75–83. (2020)

22. Regateiro, J., Boyer, E.: 3D Human Shape Style Transfer. arXiv preprint arXiv:2109.01587 (2021)

23. Jing, Y., Yang, Y., Feng, Z., Ye, J., Yu, Y., Song, M.: Neural style transfer: a review. IEEE Trans. Visual Comput. Graph. **26**, 3365–3385 (2019)

24. Li, C., Wand, M.: Precomputed real-time texture synthesis with markovian generative adversarial networks. In: Leibe, B., Matas, J., Sebe, N., Welling, M. (eds.) ECCV 2016. LNCS, vol. 9907, pp. 702–716. Springer, Cham (2016). https://doi.org/10.1007/978-3-319-46487-9_43

FSVM: Federated Support Vector Machines for Smart City

Lichuan Ma[1(✉)], Lizhen Tang[1], Longxiang Gao[2], Qingqi Pei[1], and Ming Ding[3]

[1] Shannxi Key Laboratory of Blockchain and Secure Computing, Xidian University,
Xi'an, China
lcma@xidian.edu.cn, lztang@stu.xidian.edu.cn, qqpei@mail.xidian.edu.cn
[2] Qilu University, Jinan, China
gaolx@sdas.org
[3] Information Privacy and Security Group, Data61, Commonwealth Scientific and
Industrial Research Organization, Silicon Valley, Australia
ming.ding@data61.csiro.au

Abstract. By putting digital technology and vast volume of data together, smart city becomes an emerging city paradigm for intelligent city management and operation. As one of the most popular artificial intelligent algorithms, support vector machines (SVMs) have been widely adopted for classification in various smart city applications. Due to the explosion of data and rigorous privacy requirements, an SVM classifier needs to be trained in a distributed and privacy-preserving manner. To achieve this, a federated SVM (FSVM) scheme is proposed to collaboratively and privately train an SVM classifier by combining the alternating direction method of multipliers (ADMM) with secret sharing. Specifically, the FSVM consists of FSVM-C and FSVM-S to deal with two cases of data partitioning by examples and features, respectively. By implementing the FSVM scheme on the real-word dataset MNIST, the efficiency and effectiveness of both FSVM-S and FSVM-C are verified by comprehensive experimental results.

Keywords: Federated Support Vector Machines · Privacy Preserving · ADMM

1 Introduction

Benefiting from the prevalence of cloud computing, IoT, and artificial intelligence (AI), smart city has become an emerging future city paradigm for intelligent city management and operation by putting vast volume of data and digital technology together [1]. For making better decisions, various AI algorithms, such as machine learning and deep learning algorithms, are adopted. As one of the most widely utilized AI algorithms, support vector machines (SVMs) have gained popularity in many typical smart city applications, such as fraud detection [2], disease diagnosis [3], and cyber security situation prediction [4].

© ICST Institute for Computer Sciences, Social Informatics and Telecommunications Engineering 2023
Published by Springer Nature Switzerland AG 2023. All Rights Reserved
S. Yu et al. (Eds.): TridentCom 2022, LNICST 489, pp. 149–167, 2023.
https://doi.org/10.1007/978-3-031-33458-0_11

Generally, SVM-based smart city applications rely on a centralized cloud server for gathering training data and obtaining the classifier by solving a convex optimization problem. However, due to the pervasive implementation of IoTs, the amount of data to be gathered explode and thus heavy burdens on bandwidth have been introduced for gathering these data. To tackle this problem, one new computing paradigm, namely edge computing, comes up and many smart city applications have been built on this paradigm [5]. Here, raw training data are distributed across different entities and the derivation of an SVM classifier needs their collaboration. However, privacy concerns might hinder such kind of collaboration as locally held data may include sensitive information about the holders [6]. Situations become much worse with the enforcement of a series of privacy laws including the General Data Protection Regulation by the European Union and the California Consumer Privacy Act by the US [7]. As a result, SVM classifiers should be derived in a distributed and privacy-preserving manner for current smart city applications.

For deriving SVM classifiers in a distributed manner, the authors of [8] present a method based on the alternating direction method of multipliers (ADMM). In this solution, the centralized SVM problem is split into a set of convex subproblems (one per participant) with consensus constraints on the classifier parameters. Via this solution, there is no need to exchange locally held training data and the privacy problem is addressed to some extent. Unfortunately, the method in [8] only considers the case of data partitioning by examples and it restricts the wide adoption of this method as there are many application scenarios where data are partitioned by features [9]. In addition, according to [10] and [11], the intermediate states to be exchanged when running ADMM still reveal sensitive information about the locally held training data.

To further protect the intermediate states, two types of solutions are offered by [10] and [11]. In [10], controllable noises are added to the intermediated sates such that the requirements of differential privacy are satisfied. As additional noises are introduced, the privacy goal is achieved with sacrificing accuracy. Even though the tradeoff between privacy and accuracy is explored by the authors, the speed for converging to the optimal classifier would be always decreased. By proposing a new ADMM algorithm that allows time-varying penalty matrices, the partially homomorphic encryption scheme is incorporated to protect the intermediate states in [11]. Here, the accuracy is not sacrificed but heavy computation overhead is introduced. Moreover, all the methods in [8,10] and [11] only consider the case of data partitioning by examples and it makes their adoptions to be restricted.

Thus in this paper, to conquer the drawbacks of existing works and derive SVM classifiers in a distributed and privacy-preserving manner, the federated SVM (FSVM) scheme is proposed in this paper. Here, the term "federated" is borrowed from federated learning where multiple data holders collaborate in solving a machine learning problem based on locally stored raw data without compromising data privacy [12]. The contributions of our work are summarized as following.

- Firstly, we present the system model for the proposed FSVM scheme where the general optimization problems for the cases of data partitioning by examples and features are offered for deriving SVM classifiers.
- Then, for the case of data partitioning by examples, the FSVM-C is proposed by incorporating secret sharing with the new ADMM in [11] that allows time-varying matrices. By doing this, the privacy-preserving goal can be achieved in a more efficient manner without introducing a trusted third-party for generating keys.
- After that, the FSVM-S is put forward to deal with the case of data partitioning by features. Here, we derive the closed form of the ADMM iterations that converge to the optimal solution to construct SVM classifiers. The Shamir secret sharing is introduced for protecting the intermediate states that are required to exchanged.
- By implementing the FSVM scheme on the real-word dataset MNIST, the efficiency and effectiveness of both FSVM-S and FSVM-C are verified by comprehensive experimental results.

The rest of the paper is organized as following. The preliminaries for ADMM and secret sharing are offered in Sect. 2. In Sect. 3, the FSVM system model is present. Sections 4 and 5 elaborate FSVM-C and FSVM-S for the cases of data partitioning by examples and features, respectively. Comprehensive experimental results are demonstrated in Sect. 6 to verify the efficiency and effectiveness of the proposed scheme. At the end, Sect. 7 concludes this paper.

2   Preliminaries

In this section, we offer a simple introduction to two building blocks of the proposed FSVM scheme. One is the ADMM algorithm by which global SVM classifiers can be derived without requiring to collect all the training data together. The other is the secret sharing that enables to preserve the privacy of intermediate parameters (or states) when multiple data holders collaboratively run the ADMM algorithm.

2.1   The ADMM Algorithm

Since most machine learning models are derived by solving large-scale convex optimizations problems, there is an urgent need to put forward efficient algorithms to solve these problems. Fortunately, the ADMM algorithm is one of the popular solutions. By splitting the original problems into several sub-problems, this algorithm makes it possible to solve large-scale convex optimizations in a distributed manner. When moving to current smart city scenarios where raw training data are held by multiple entities, ADMM-based solutions offer an efficient way to train a more accurate model via their collaboration. Moreover, raw training data are locally kept when running this algorithm. Thus in the proposed FSVM scheme, the ADMM algorithm is adopted for multiple data holders to train a global SVM classifier.

As in [9], the optimization problem to solved is in the following format

$$\min \ f(\boldsymbol{x}) + g(\boldsymbol{z}) \quad s.t. \quad \boldsymbol{Ax} + \boldsymbol{Bz} = \boldsymbol{c} \tag{1}$$

Authors of [9] offer the solution for this problem as

$$\boldsymbol{x}^{k+1} := \mathrm{argmin}_{\boldsymbol{x}} L_\rho(\boldsymbol{x}, \boldsymbol{z}^k, \boldsymbol{y}^k) \tag{2}$$

$$\boldsymbol{z}^{k+1} := \mathrm{argmin}_{\boldsymbol{z}} L_\rho(\boldsymbol{x}^{k+1}, \boldsymbol{z}, \boldsymbol{y}^k) \tag{3}$$

$$\boldsymbol{y}^{k+1} := \boldsymbol{y}^k + \rho(\boldsymbol{Ax}^{k+1} + \boldsymbol{Bz}^{k+1} - \boldsymbol{c}) \tag{4}$$

where L_ρ is the augmented Lagrangian. By iteratively computing (basic-solution-1) (basic-solution-3), $\boldsymbol{x}^k$ and $\boldsymbol{z}^k$ converge to the optimal solution to the problem defined by (1). Here, $\boldsymbol{x}$ and $\boldsymbol{z}$ are updated alternatively and this accounts for the term *alternating direction*. By introducing the dual variable $\boldsymbol{y}$, the minimization of $\boldsymbol{x}$ and $\boldsymbol{z}$ are separated and this equips the ADMM algorithm with the property of being run in a distributed manner.

2.2   Secret Sharing

Secret sharing schemes serve as the foundation for most of state-of-the-art privacy preserving techniques [13]. These schemes are suitable for multiple parties with comparable capabilities to collaboratively evaluate a variety of functions without revealing their own inputs to others. The main advantage of these schemes is that their implementations do not rely on any trusted third-party. According to [14], there are two categories of secret sharing schemes, namely arithmetic sharing and boolean sharing.

With respect to arithmetic sharing, the first scheme is referred as Shamir Secret Sharing, where the shares are the points of a polynomial [15]. Specifically, given a value s that a party want to share with other parties, the shares of s, denoted by $\{\langle s \rangle_1^A, \ldots, \langle s \rangle_n^A\}$ are computed as following

- The holder of s randomly picks a polynomial function $f(x) \in_r \mathbb{F}_p$ that satisfies $f(0) = s$.
- This holder randomly chooses s_i $(i = 1, \ldots, n)$ from $\mathbb{F}_p$ and computes $f(s_i)$. By this way, the i-th share of s is a tuple $\langle s \rangle_i^A = (s_i, f(s_i))$.

Note that, the degree of $f(x)$ determines the least number of shareholders required to reconstruct s. Let t denote the degree of $f(x)$ and at least $t + 1$ shareholders are needed for the reconstruction. Therefore, given $k > t$, the reconstruction can be done via

$$s = \sum_{i=1}^{k} f(s_i) \left(\prod_{j=1, j \neq i}^{k} \frac{s_j}{s_i - s_i} \right) mod(p) \tag{5}$$

When there are only two parties, such sharing becomes the form that is proposed in [14]. Arithmetic sharing has been proved to be efficient to collaboratively privately evaluate functions containing arithmetic operations, like additions and multiplications.

As for boolean sharing, it is usually utilized in the two-party case. Here, the secret to be shared is represented by its binary format and each of the bits is shared via XOR-operations. Given the secret s to be shared, its binary format is $[s_1, \ldots, s_l]$. For the i-th bit s_i, its boolean shares, $\langle s_i \rangle_0^B$ and $\langle s_i \rangle_0^B$, are generated by

- The holder of s randomly chooses one bit r from $\{0, 1\}$ and set $\langle s_i \rangle_0^B = r$ that is kept by himself.
- This holder sets $\langle s_i \rangle_1^B = s_i \oplus r$ and sends $\langle s_i \rangle_1^B$ to the other party.

To reconstruct s, it is just needed to compute $\langle s_i \rangle_0^B \oplus \langle s_i \rangle_1^B$. The types of operations tackled by boolean sharing are XOR and AND. Thus, boolean sharing is good at privately evaluating functions that mainly contain comparison operation. For further details, we refer the readers to [14].

3   System Model

For traditional SVMs, all the data entries are collected and trained to derive a classification model by a centralized server. Assume there are M data entries. For the i-th entry, we have $x_i \in R^D$ and the label $y_i \in \{-1, 1\}$. Let ξ denote the vector of slack variables. The goal is to obtain the classification model as a maximum-margin linear discriminant function $g^* = x^T \omega^* + b^*$ by solving the following convex optimization problem

$$\min_{\omega, b, \xi} \frac{1}{2} \|\omega\|^2 + C \sum_{i=1}^{M} \xi_i \tag{6}$$
$$s.t. \quad y_i(\omega x_i + b) \geq 1 - \xi_i, \quad \xi_i \geq 0 \quad (i = 1, \cdots, M)$$

Since in many smart city applications, training data are from different data holders and they collaborate with each other to obtain a more accurate classification model. Assume that there are N participants to act as data holders in the system model for the proposed FSVM scheme. For the i-th participant, the number of data entries that he holds is assumed to be M_i and X_i is the matrix that stores these data entries. Let x_{ij} and y_{ij} $(j = 1, \ldots, M_i)$ be the j-th data entry and the corresponding label, respectively. Here, $y_{ij} \in \{-1, 1\}$. In addition, the total number of features that are considered in our scheme is D. As stated in [12], when referring to the scenario where multiple data holders collaboratively train a model, there are two types of data partitioning conditions, namely partitioning by examples and partitioning by features. Thus in the proposed FSVM scheme, two cases related to the different data partitioning conditions should be considered.

The first one is related to data partitioning by examples. This means that the data entries of each participant have the same number of features. Thus,

$\boldsymbol{X}_i \in \mathbb{R}^{M_i \times D}$ and $\boldsymbol{x}_{ij}^T \in \mathbb{R}^D$ $(i = 1, \ldots, N)$. The superscript T means transposition. Here, to collaboratively obtain the maximum-margin linear discriminant function, the optimization problem to be solved changes from the one defined by (6) to

$$\min_{\boldsymbol{\omega}_i, b_i, \xi_{i,j}} \frac{1}{2} \sum_{i=1}^{N} \|\boldsymbol{\omega}_i\|^2 + NC \sum_{i=1}^{N} \sum_{j=1}^{M_i} \xi_{ij}$$

$$s.t. \begin{cases} y_{ij}(\boldsymbol{x}_{ij}\boldsymbol{\omega}_i + b_i) \geq 1 - \xi_{ij}, & \xi_{ij} \geq 0 \\ (i = 1, \cdots, N, \ j = 1, \cdots, M_i) \\ \boldsymbol{\omega}_i = \boldsymbol{\omega}_k, b_i = b_k(i, k = 1, \ldots, N \text{ and } i \neq k) \end{cases} \tag{7}$$

Here, $\boldsymbol{\omega}_i \in \mathbb{R}^D$ $(i = 1, \ldots, N)$. After solving (7), each participant obtains the same $\boldsymbol{\omega}^*$ and b^*. This is also named consensus-based SVM [8]. For simplicity, the proposed FSVM scheme for this case is denoted by FSVM-C.

The second case is related to data partitioning by features. Here, each participant has the same number of data entries but the number of features of each entry is different. An example for this case is when different companies that have an overlapping set of customers and they collaborate to derive a global classifier that takes richer features into consideration. Let D_i denote the number of data features that the i-th participant holds. We have $M_1 = \cdots = M_N = M$, $\sum_{i=1}^{N} D_i = D$, $\boldsymbol{X}_i \in \mathbb{R}^{M \times D_i}$ and $\boldsymbol{x}_{ij} \in \mathbb{R}^{D_i}$.

$$\min_{\boldsymbol{\omega}_i, b_i, \xi_{i,j}} \frac{1}{2} \sum_{i=1}^{N} \|\boldsymbol{\omega}_i\|^2 + \sum_{j=1}^{M} \xi_j$$

$$s.t. \begin{cases} y_j \sum_{i=1}^{N}(\boldsymbol{x}_{ij}\boldsymbol{\omega}_i + b_i) \geq 1 - \xi_j, & \xi_j \geq 0 \\ (j = 1, \cdots, M) \end{cases} \tag{8}$$

Here, $\boldsymbol{\omega}_i \in \mathbb{R}^{D_i}$ $(i = 1, \ldots, N)$. Following [9], this is the sharing-based SVM and the proposed FSVM scheme for this case is called FSVM-S.

Considering the definition of threat model, we assume that all the enrolled participants in the proposed FSVM scheme are semi-honest. This implies that these participants act honestly following the proposed scheme but are curious about what they have received from other participants. In addition, it is assumed that there are no colluding participants. The same as [10] and [11], the privacy preserving goal is to protect both the raw data and intermediate parameters (i.e. the output of each iteration when adopting the ADMM algorithm) against semi-honest collaborators when solving the problems defined by (7) and (8).

4   The Proposed FSVM-C Scheme

As in this paper, the proposed FSVM scheme contains the FSVM-C and FSVM-S for data partitioning by examples and features, respectively. In this section, we first explicitly present how FSVM-C works.

4.1   Problem Reformulation

Following [8], the problem defined by (7) that is solved by FSVM-C in a privacy-preserving manner can be reformulated into a more compact form. Set $v_i = [\boldsymbol{\omega}_i^T, b_i]^T \in \mathbb{R}^{D+1}$, $\boldsymbol{B}_i = [\boldsymbol{X}_i, \boldsymbol{1}_i]$ $(\boldsymbol{1}_i \in \mathbb{R}^{M_i})$, $\boldsymbol{Y}_i = diag([y_{i1}, \cdots, y_{iM_i}])$, and $\boldsymbol{\xi}_i = [\xi_{i1}, \cdots, \xi_{iM_i}]^T \in \mathbb{R}^{M_i}$. Moreover, let $\boldsymbol{I}_{D+1}$ be the identity matrix of dimension $D+1$ and $\boldsymbol{\Pi}_{D+1} \in \mathbb{R}^{(D+1) \times (D+1)}$ be a matrix of zeros except $\boldsymbol{\Pi}_{D+1, D+1} = 1$. The more compact form of the optimization problem defined by (7) becomes

$$\min_{v_i, \boldsymbol{\xi}_i} \frac{1}{2} \sum_{i=1}^{N} v_i^T (\boldsymbol{I}_{D+1} - \boldsymbol{\Pi}_{D+1}) v_i + NC \sum_{i=1}^{N} \boldsymbol{1}_i^T \boldsymbol{\xi}_i \tag{9}$$

$$s.t. \quad \begin{cases} \boldsymbol{Y}_i \boldsymbol{B}_i \boldsymbol{V}_i \succeq \boldsymbol{1}_i - \boldsymbol{\xi}_i, & \boldsymbol{\xi}_i \succeq \boldsymbol{0}_i (\forall i) \\ \boldsymbol{A} \boldsymbol{V} = 0 \end{cases}$$

Here, $\boldsymbol{V} = [v_1^T, \ldots, v_N^T]^T \in \mathbb{R}^{N(D+1)}$. As for $\boldsymbol{A} \in \mathbb{R}^{N(D+1) \times (N-1)(D+1)}$, it is defined as

$$\boldsymbol{A} = \begin{bmatrix} \boldsymbol{I}_{D+1} & -\boldsymbol{I}_{D+1} & 0 & \cdots & 0 \\ \vdots & \vdots & \vdots & \ddots & \ddots \\ 0 & 0 & \cdots & \boldsymbol{I}_{D+1} & -\boldsymbol{I}_{D+1} \end{bmatrix}$$

Note that $\boldsymbol{A}$ is introduced to settle down the constraints $\boldsymbol{\omega}_i = \boldsymbol{\omega}_k$ and $b_i = b_k$ $(i, k = 1, \ldots, N$ and $i \neq k)$ in (7).

To solve the optimization problem defined by (9), the authors of [11] offer an ADMM-based solution with time-varying penalty matrices as

$$\{v_i^{k+1}, \boldsymbol{\xi}_i^{k+1}\} = \arg\min_{v_i, \boldsymbol{\xi}_i} L(v_i, \boldsymbol{\xi}_i, \rho^k, \lambda^k) + \frac{r_i}{2} \|v_i - v_i^k\|^2 \tag{10}$$

$$\rho^k \to \rho^{k+1} \tag{11}$$

$$\lambda_{i,i+1}^{k+1} = \lambda_{i,i+1}^k + \rho_{i,i+1}^{k+1} (v_i^{k+1} - v_{i+1}^{k+1}) \tag{12}$$

where $L(v, \boldsymbol{\xi}, \boldsymbol{\lambda}, \boldsymbol{\rho})$ is the augmented surrogate. Lagrangian function that is defined as

$$L(v, \boldsymbol{\xi}, \boldsymbol{\lambda}, \boldsymbol{\rho}) = \frac{1}{2} \sum_{i=1}^{N} v_i^T (\boldsymbol{I}_{D+1} - \boldsymbol{\Pi}_{D+1}) v_i + NC \sum_{i=1}^{N} \boldsymbol{1}_i^T \boldsymbol{\xi}_i$$

$$+ \sum_{i=1}^{N-1} (\boldsymbol{\lambda}_{i,i+1}^T (v_i - v_{i+1}) + \frac{\rho_{i,i+1}}{2} \|v_i - v_{i+1}\|^2) \tag{13}$$

As for the set of penalties $\boldsymbol{\rho}$, the following two requirements guarantee the convergence to optimal solutions

$$0 \preccurlyeq \rho^k \preccurlyeq \rho^{k+1} \preccurlyeq \bar{\rho} \tag{14}$$

$$Q_P + \boldsymbol{I}_{ND} \succcurlyeq \boldsymbol{A}^T \bar{\rho} \boldsymbol{A} \tag{15}$$

Here, $\boldsymbol{Q}_P = diag\{r_1, \ldots, r_N\} \otimes \boldsymbol{I}_D \in \mathbb{R}^{ND \times ND}$ ($\otimes$ refers to the Kronecker product).

From the iterated solution above, (10) can be locally solved by each enrolled participant and this is the key to form a distributed solution. Even though the locally hold data need not to be exchanged among the participants, the intermediate state $\boldsymbol{v}_i$ after each iteration should be sent to others when locally solving (10). This violates the privacy-preserving requirements as such intermediate states might reveal sensitive information related the locally hold data [10,11].

To protect $\boldsymbol{v}_i$ after each iteration, each penalty $\rho_{i,i+1}^k$ ($i = 1, \ldots, N-1$) for iteration k is constructed as the multiplication of q_i and q_{i+1} which are secretly hold by the i-th and j-th participants, respectively. By introducing the homomorphic encryption scheme, the locally computed $\boldsymbol{v}_i$ and $\boldsymbol{v}_{i+1}^k$ are masked when computing $\rho_{i,i+1}^k(\boldsymbol{v}_i - \boldsymbol{v}_{i+1})$. Due to the limited number operations that can be supported by homomorphic encryption and the heavy computation overhead, we proposed a more efficient solution, namely FSVM-C, which is built upon the ADMM-based solution with time-varying penalty matrices.

4.2   The FSVM-C Scheme

To depict how the proposed FSVM-C works, we focus on the operations of i-th participant. For the $(k+1)$-th iteration, the first for this participant is to solve the optimization problem defined by (10). According to the formulation of the augmented surrogate Lagrangian function in (13), $\boldsymbol{v}_i^{k+1}$ satisfies

$$\nabla_{\boldsymbol{v}_i}(L(\boldsymbol{v}, \boldsymbol{\xi}, \boldsymbol{\lambda}, \boldsymbol{\rho}) + \frac{r_i}{2}\|\boldsymbol{v}_i - \boldsymbol{v}_i^k\|^2) = 0 \qquad (16)$$

Following the $\boldsymbol{\lambda}$-update in (11), $\boldsymbol{\lambda}_{i-1,i}^k$ and $\boldsymbol{\lambda}_{i,i+1}^k$ are computed as

$$\boldsymbol{\lambda}_{i-1,i}^k = \boldsymbol{\lambda}_{i-1,i}^{k-1} + \rho_{i-1,i}^k(\boldsymbol{v}_{i-1} - \boldsymbol{v}_{i+1}) \qquad (17)$$

$$\boldsymbol{\lambda}_{i,i+1}^k = \boldsymbol{\lambda}_{i,i+1}^{k-1} + \rho_{i,i+1}^k(\boldsymbol{v}_i - \boldsymbol{v}_{i+1}) \qquad (18)$$

From (16), (17), and (18), it is explicit that the i-th participant needs to collect $\boldsymbol{v}_{i-1}^k$ and $\boldsymbol{v}_{i+1}^k$ to solve the equation in (16) to obtain $\boldsymbol{v}_i^{k+1}$. Considering the privacy-preserving goal, $\boldsymbol{v}_{i-1}^k$ and $\boldsymbol{v}_{i+1}^k$ should not be exposed to the i-th participant. In the following, we show how to achieve this in a more efficient manner compared to [11]. Without loss of generality, we show the detailed process for computing $\rho_{i,i+1}^k(\boldsymbol{v}_{i+1}^k - \boldsymbol{v}_i^k)$ without revealing $\boldsymbol{v}_{i+1}^k$ and $\boldsymbol{v}_i^k$ to each other. As for computing $\rho_{i-1,i}^k(\boldsymbol{v}_{i-1}^k - \boldsymbol{v}_i^k)$, the privacy-preserving goal can be achieved in the same manner.

In [11], $\rho_{i,i+1}^k$ is constructed as $\rho_{i,i+1}^k = q_{i,i+1}^k \cdot q_{i+1,i}^k$ where $q_{i,i+1}^k$ and $q_{i+1,i}^k$ are privately held by the i-th and j-th participants, respectively. With the help of the additional homomorphic encryption scheme, $\rho_{i-1,i}^k(\boldsymbol{v}_{i+1}^k - \boldsymbol{v}_i^k)$ can be derived while keeping $\boldsymbol{v}_{i+1}^k$ and $\boldsymbol{v}_i^k$ secret. However, this kind of method introduces heavy computation overhead. In the proposed FSVM-C scheme, we split $\rho_{i,i+1}^k$ as $\rho_{i,i+1}^k = q_{i,i+1}^k + q_{i+1,i}^k$ and propose a new off-line protocol to securely generate $q_{i,i+1}^k$ and $q_{i+1,i}^k$. Then, the algorithm to solve the optimization problem defined by (7) in an efficient and privacy-preserving manner is given.

To satisfying the conditions of (14) and (15) for ρ-update, we have the following observations

- For r_i ($i = 1, \ldots, N$), they are predefined and public parameters and their values are kept unchanged during the iterations for deriving the optimal solution.
- When focusing on the i-th participant, $\rho_{i,i+1}^k \leq \rho_{i,i+1}^{k+1}$ and the upper bound is determined by r_i.
- Once r_i is determined, a series of $\rho_{i,i+1}$ can be derived to satisfying the conditions of (14) and (15) and this process is independent from the iterations to derive the optimal solution.

From this observation, for the i-th and $i + 1$-th participants, they should collaboratively generate two sequences of $\{q_{i,i+1}^k\}$ and $\{q_{i+1,i}^k\}$ that the sequence of $\{q_{i,i+1}^k + q_{i+1,i}^k\}$ is in an ascending order as k increases. Let Q denotes the size of such sequence and Q is large enough for the iterations of (10)–(12) converging to an optimal solution. The basic idea for generating these two sequences is that these two participants first generate two random sequences of size $Q + 1$, namely $q_{i,i+1}$ and $q_{i+1,i}$, and then rearrange these two sequences such that $\{q_{i+1,i}^k + q_{i+1,i}^k\}$ is in an ascending order as k increases. The core operation in this process, referred as CMP, is to compare $q_{i,i+1}^k + q_{i+1,i}^k$ and $q_{i,i+1}^{k+1} + q_{i+1,i}^{k+1}$ without exposing $q_{i,i+1}^k$, $q_{i,i+1}^{k+1}$, $q_{i+1,i}^k$ and $q_{i+1,i}^{k+1}$ to the other party.

In the following, we elaborate how to achieve the function of CMP.

- **Step 1**: For the i-th participant, he transforms $q_{i,i+1}^k$ to its l-bit binary denotation as $[q_{i,i+1}^k]$. Then, two l-bit binary numbers, $\langle q_{i,i+1}^k \rangle_1^B$ and $\langle q_{i,i+1}^k \rangle_2^B$ are randomly selected such that

$$[q_{i,i+1}^k] = \langle q_{i,i+1}^k \rangle_1^B \oplus \langle q_{i,i+1}^k \rangle_2^B$$

where $\oplus$ denotes the XOR operation. Here, $\langle q_{i,i+1}^k \rangle_1^B$ and $\langle q_{i,i+1}^k \rangle_2^B$ are the boolean shares of $[q_{i,i+1}^k]$. In the same manner, the boolean shares of $q_{i,i+1}^{k+1}$, $q_{i+1,i}^k$ and $q_{i+1,i}^{k+1}$ are generated.
- **Step 2**: Before utilizing boolean shares to privately compare $q_{i,i+1}^k + q_{i+1,i}^k$ and $q_{i,i+1}^{k+1} + q_{i+1,i}^{k+1}$, we need to construct the corresponding boolean circuits beforehand. Here, the improved boolean circuits for addition and comparison proposed by [16] are introduced. Figure 1 shows the boolean circuit for the CMP operation.
- **Step 3**: Following the process shown in Fig. 1, the i-th and $i+1$-th generated the shares of the final comparison result. After exchanging the shares, these two participants finally obtain the comparison result. For the detailed process, we refer the readers to [16].

With the help of CMP operation, the i-th and $i + 1$-th participants can generate $\{q_{i,i+1}^k\}$ and $\{q_{i+1,i}^k\}$ (of size $Q + 1$) such that $\{q_{i,i+1}^k + q_{i+1,i}^k\}$ is in an

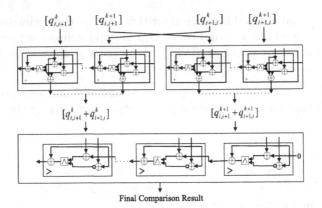

Fig. 1. The boolean circuit for CMP operation

ascending order. $q_{i,i+1}^{Q+1}$ and $q_{i+1,i}^{Q+1}$ are published and $q_{i,i+1}^{Q+1} + q_{i+1,i}^{Q+1}$ is utilized to generate $\boldsymbol{Q}_P$ satisfying the condition of (15).

For the k-th iteration, given $\{q_{i,i+1}^k\}$ and $\{q_{i+1,i}^k\}$, the i-th and $i+1$-th participants privately derive $\rho_{i,i+1}^k(\boldsymbol{v}_{i+1}^k - \boldsymbol{v}_i^k)$ by the following procedures

- **Step 1:** For the i-th participant, $\langle q_{i,i+1}^k \rangle_1^A$ and $\langle q_{i,i+1}^k \rangle_2^A$ are randomly selected such that $\langle q_{i,i+1}^k \rangle_1^A + \langle q_{i,i+1}^k \rangle_2^A = q_{i,i+1}^k$. Here, $\langle q_{i,i+1}^k \rangle_1^A$ and $\langle q_{i,i+1}^k \rangle_2^A$ are the arithmetic shares of $q_{i,i+1}^k$. Then, the arithmetic shares of $-\boldsymbol{v}_i^k$ and $-q_{i,i+1}\boldsymbol{v}_i^k$, namely $\langle -\boldsymbol{v}_i^k \rangle_1^A$, $\langle -\boldsymbol{v}_i^k \rangle_2^A$, $\langle -q_{i,i+1}\boldsymbol{v}_i^k \rangle_1^A$ and $\langle -q_{i,i+1}\boldsymbol{v}_i^k \rangle_2^A$, are generated. $\langle q_{i,i+1}^k \rangle_2^A$, $\langle -\boldsymbol{v}_i^k \rangle_2^A$, and $\langle -q_{i,i+1}\boldsymbol{v}_i^k \rangle_2^A$ are sent to the $i+1$-th participant.
- **Step 2:** By the same way, the $i+1$-th participant generates $\langle q_{i+1,i}^k \rangle_1^A$, $\langle q_{i+1,i}^k \rangle_2^A$, $\langle \boldsymbol{v}_{i+1}^k \rangle_1^A$, $\langle \boldsymbol{v}_{i+1}^k \rangle_2^A$, $\langle q_{i+1,i}^k \boldsymbol{v}_{i+1}^k \rangle_1^A$ and $\langle q_{i+1,i}^k \boldsymbol{v}_{i+1}^k \rangle_2^A$. $\langle q_{i+1,i}^k \rangle_1^A$, $\langle \boldsymbol{v}_{i+1}^k \rangle_1^A$ and $\langle q_{i+1,i}^k \boldsymbol{v}_{i+1}^k \rangle_1^A$ are sent to the i-th participant.
- **Step 3:** Given $\langle q_{i+1,i}^k \rangle_1^A$, the i-th participant can locally compute its share of $-q_{i+1,i}^k \boldsymbol{v}_i^k$ and $q_{i,i+1}^k \boldsymbol{v}_{i+1}^k$, referred to $\langle -q_{i+1,i}^k \boldsymbol{v}_i^k \rangle_1^A$ and $\langle q_{i,i+1}^k \boldsymbol{v}_{i+1}^k \rangle_1^A$, with the help of pre-computed multiplication triple [17]. Then, $\langle (q_{i,i+1}^k + q_{i+1,i}^k)(\boldsymbol{v}_{i+1}^k - \boldsymbol{v}_i^k) \rangle_1^A$ is derived by

$$\langle (q_{i,i+1}^k + q_{i+1,i}^k)(\boldsymbol{v}_{i+1}^k - \boldsymbol{v}_i^k) \rangle_1^A = \langle q_{i+1,i}^k \boldsymbol{v}_{i+1}^k \rangle_1^A q_{i,i+1}^k \boldsymbol{v}_{i+1}^k \rangle_1^A$$
$$+ \langle -q_{i+1,i}^k \boldsymbol{v}_i^k \rangle_1^A + \langle -q_{i,i+1}\boldsymbol{v}_i^k \rangle_1^A$$

Similarly, the $i+1$-th participant is capable of locally computing $\langle (q_{i,i+1}^k + q_{i+1,i}^k)(\boldsymbol{v}_{i+1}^k - \boldsymbol{v}_i^k) \rangle_2^A$

- **Step 4:** Finally, these two participants exchange $\langle (q_{i,i+1}^k + q_{i+1,i}^k)(\boldsymbol{v}_{i+1}^k - \boldsymbol{v}_i^k) \rangle_1^A$ and $\langle (q_{i,i+1}^k + q_{i+1,i}^k)(\boldsymbol{v}_{i+1}^k - \boldsymbol{v}_i^k) \rangle_2^A$ to reconstruct $\rho_{i,i+1}(\boldsymbol{v}_{i+1}^k - \boldsymbol{v}_i^k) = (q_{i,i+1}^k + q_{i+1,i}^k)(\boldsymbol{v}_{i+1}^k - \boldsymbol{v}_i^k) = \langle (q_{i,i+1}^k + q_{i+1,i}^k)(\boldsymbol{v}_{i+1}^k - \boldsymbol{v}_i^k) \rangle_1^A + \langle (q_{i,i+1}^k + q_{i+1,i}^k)(\boldsymbol{v}_{i+1}^k - \boldsymbol{v}_i^k) \rangle_2^A$. Note that all the computations here are all mod 2^l.

After securely computing $\rho_{i,i+1}^k(v_{i+1}^k - v_i^k)$, utilizing the iterations of (10)–(12) to find the optimal solution will not reveal the intermediate state of each enrolled participant. Even though the proposed method introduces more interactions, they can be pre-computed and the heavy computation overhead introduced by homomorphic encryptions in [11] can be dramatically reduced.

5   The Proposed FSVM-S Scheme

To collaboratively train a SVM classifier with privacy concerns for the case of data partitioning by features, the FSVM-S scheme is proposed here. Like Sect. 4, we begin with reformulating the optimization problem defined by (8) to a more compact form. After that, the ADMM-based solution is presented. Even though locally held data are not required to be exchanged by such a solution, intermediate states still reveal sensitive information of raw data. Thus, the Shamir secret sharing scheme is introduced to protect such intermediate states.

5.1   Problem Reformulation

Similar to the FSVM-C scheme, we first reformulate the problem defined by (8) to make it easier to derive an ADMM-based solution. Let $(x)_+$ denote the function that $(x)_+ = \max\{0, x\}$. By introducing such a function, the slack variables can be eliminated and (8) becomes

$$\min \sum_{i=1}^N \frac{1}{2}\|\boldsymbol{\omega}_i\|^2 + \mathbf{1}_M^T(\mathbf{1}_M - \boldsymbol{Y}\sum_{i=1}^M(\boldsymbol{X}_i\boldsymbol{\omega}_i + b_i\mathbf{1}_M))_+ \tag{19}$$

where $\boldsymbol{Y} = diag[y_1, \ldots, y_M]$. In the sequel, set $\boldsymbol{v}_i = [[\boldsymbol{\omega}_i^T], b_i]^T \in \boldsymbol{R}^{D_i+1}$ and $\boldsymbol{B}_i = [\boldsymbol{X}_i^T, \mathbf{1}_M] \in \boldsymbol{R}^{M\times(D_i+1)}$. As a result, the problem of (19) is further transformed to

$$\min \quad \sum_{i=1}^N \frac{1}{2}\boldsymbol{v}_i^T(\boldsymbol{I}_{D_i+1} - \boldsymbol{\Pi}_{D_i+1})\boldsymbol{v}_i$$
$$+ \mathbf{1}_M^T(\mathbf{1}_M - \boldsymbol{Y}\sum_{i=1}^N \boldsymbol{B}_i\boldsymbol{v}_i)_+ \tag{20}$$

Recalling the standard problem defined by (1) that is solved by the ADMM algorithm, we introduce additional variables $\boldsymbol{z}_i \in \mathbb{R}^M$ $(i = 1, \ldots, N)$ to enable a distributed algorithm for solving the problem of (20). To achieve this, we put the constraint on $\boldsymbol{z}_i$ that $\boldsymbol{z}_i = \boldsymbol{B}_i\boldsymbol{v}_i$. Consequently, the problem defined by (20) is transformed to

$$\min \quad \sum_{i=1}^N \frac{1}{2}\boldsymbol{v}_i^T(\boldsymbol{I}_{D_i+1} - \boldsymbol{\Pi}_{D_i+1})\boldsymbol{v}_i + \mathbf{1}_M^T(\mathbf{1}_M - \boldsymbol{Y}\sum_{i=1}^N \boldsymbol{z}_i)_+ \tag{21}$$
$$s.t. \quad \boldsymbol{z}_i = \boldsymbol{B}_i\boldsymbol{v}_i, \, i = 1, \ldots, N$$

By doing this, the augmented Lagrangian for (21) becomes

$$
\begin{aligned}
L_\rho &= \sum_{i=1}^{N} \frac{1}{2} v_i^T (I_{D_i+1} - \Pi_{D_i+1}) v_i + 1_M^T (1_M - Y \sum_{i=1}^{N} z_i)_+ \\
&\quad + \sum_{i=1}^{N} s_i^T (B_i v_i - z_i) + \frac{\rho}{2} \sum_{i=1}^{N} \|z_i - B_i v_i\|^2 \\
&= \sum_{i=1}^{N} f(v_i) + g(\sum_{i=1}^{N} z_i) + \sum_{i=1}^{N} s_i^T (B_i v_i - z_i) \\
&\quad + \frac{\rho}{2} \sum_{i=1}^{N} \|z_i - B_i v_i\|^2
\end{aligned}
\tag{22}
$$

In this way, the ADMM-based solution to the problem (21) is directed as

$$
v^{k+1} = \operatorname{argmin}_v L_\rho(v, z^k, s^k) \tag{23}
$$

$$
z^{k+1} = \operatorname{argmin}_z L_\rho(v^{k+1}, z, s^k) \tag{24}
$$

$$
s^{k+1} = s^k + \rho(\sum_{i=1}^{N} B_i v_i^{k+1} - z_i^{k+1}) \tag{25}
$$

where $z = \{z_1, \ldots, z_N\}$. Considering the z-update, there are $N \times M$ variables that increase the hardness for updating z. In the proposed FSVM-S scheme, we first simplify the process of updating z by substituting z with $\bar{z} = \sum_{i=1}^{N} z_i / N$. Then, the Shamir secret sharing scheme is introduced to protect the intermediate state of each participant.

5.2   The Proposed FSVM-S Scheme

According to (24), updating z requires to solve a minimization problem that contains $N \times M$ variables. Once the number of enrolled participants in the FSVM-S scheme is large, the solution becomes dramatically complex. Fortunately, inspired by [9], z can be substituted by $\bar{z} = \sum_{i=1}^{N} z_i / N$. In the following, we will show how to achieve this.

Following [9], we first transform the iterations of (23)–(25) to their scaled form as

$$
v_i^{k+1} = \operatorname{argmin}_{v_i} f_i(v_i) + \frac{\rho}{2} \|B_i v_i - z_i^k + u_i^k\|^2 \tag{26}
$$

$$
z^{k+1} = \arg\min_z g(\sum_{i=1}^{N} z_i) \frac{\rho}{2} \sum_{i=1}^{N} \|z_i - B_i v_i^{k+1} - u_i^k\|^2 \tag{27}
$$

$$
u_i^{k+1} = u_i^k + B_i v_i^{k+1} - z_i^{k+1} \tag{28}
$$

Focusing on (27), let $a_i^k = B_i v_i^{k+1} + u_i^k$. To update z is equivalent to solve the following optimization problem.

$$\min g(N\bar{z}) + \frac{\rho}{2}\sum_{i=1}^{N}\|z_i - a_i^k\| \quad s.t. \quad N\bar{z} = \sum_{i=1}^{N} z_i \tag{29}$$

After solving (29), for $i = 1, \ldots, N$, one can derive

$$z_i^{k+1} = a_i^k + \bar{z}^{k+1} - \bar{a}^k \tag{30}$$

where

$$\bar{a}^k = \frac{1}{N}\sum_{i=1}^{N} a_i^k = \frac{1}{N}\sum_{i=1}^{N}(B_i v_i^{k+1} + u_i^k) = \bar{u}^k + \overline{Bv}^{k+1}$$

Substituting z_i^{k+1} computed by (30) into (28) for updating u_i, we derive

$$u_i^{k+1} = \bar{a}^k - \bar{z}^{k+1} = \bar{u}^k + \overline{Bv}^{k+1} - \bar{z}^{k+1} \tag{31}$$

From (31), all the values of u_i^{k+1} ($i = 1, \ldots, N$) are the same. Hence, the iterations to derive the solution become

$$v_i^{k+1} = \arg\min_{v_i} f_i(v_i) + \frac{\rho}{2}\|B_i v_i - B_i v_i^k - \bar{z}^k + \overline{Bv}^k + u^k\|^2 \tag{32}$$

$$\bar{z}^{k+1} = \arg\min_{\bar{z}} g(N\bar{z}) + \frac{N\rho}{2}\|\bar{z} - \overline{Bv}^{k+1} - u^k\|^2 \tag{33}$$

$$u^{k+1} = u^k + \overline{Bv}^{k+1} - \bar{z}^{k+1} \tag{34}$$

After simplifying (27) to (33), one can derive the expression of $\bar{z}^{k+1}$ in the component level, i.e. $\bar{z}_j^{k+1}$ ($j = 1, \ldots, M$)

$$\bar{z}_j^{k+1} = \begin{cases} \bar{a}_j^k + y_j/\rho, & y_j\bar{a}_j^k \leq 1/N - 1/\rho \\ \frac{1}{N}, & 1/N - 1/\rho < y_j\bar{a}_j^k < 1/N \\ \bar{a}_j^k, & y_j\bar{a}_j^k \geq 1/N \end{cases} \tag{35}$$

where $\bar{a} = \overline{Bv}^{k+1} + u^k \in \mathbb{R}^M$.

After deriving the iterations to obtain the optimal solution to the problem defined by (21), the next is to analyze what intermediate states are exposed to others. From the iterations of (32)–(34), if all the participants can collaboratively compute $\overline{Bv} = \sum i = 1^N (B_i v_i)/N$, v_i ($i = 1, \ldots, N$), $\bar{z}$ and u can be locally updated by each participant in a distributed manner. Hence, in the proposed FSVM-S scheme, how to compute $\overline{Bv}$ collaboratively and privately should be thorough addressed. To achieve this, the detailed procedures are as following.

- **Step 1**: Fixing the iteration index k, the i-th participant picks a polynomial function $f_i^k(x) \in_r \mathbb{F}_p$ of degree t ($t + 1 \leq N$).

- **Step 2**: Focusing on the i-th participant $(i = 1, \ldots, N)$, $\boldsymbol{B}_i \boldsymbol{v}_i^k \in \mathbb{R}^M$ is computed. For the j-th element $(\boldsymbol{B}_i \boldsymbol{v}_i^k)_j$ $(j = 1, \ldots, M)$, set $f_i^k(0) = (\boldsymbol{B}_i \boldsymbol{v}_i)_j$. Then, generate N random values as $\{h_{ij}^1, \ldots, h_{ij}^N\}$. The shares of $(\boldsymbol{B}_i \boldsymbol{v}_i^k)_j$ can be obtained as

$$\langle (\boldsymbol{B}_i \boldsymbol{v}_i^k)_j \rangle_n = (h_{ij}^n, f_i^k(h_{ij}^n)) \quad (n = 1, \ldots, N) \tag{36}$$

This participant keeps on share by himself and sends the left $N - 1$ shares to the other participants.
- **Step 3**: After receiving the shares from the other participants, the i-th participant computes

$$\langle (N\overline{\boldsymbol{Bv}})_j^k \rangle_i = \sum_{n=1}^{N} \langle (\boldsymbol{B}_n \boldsymbol{v}_n^k)_j \rangle_i \quad (j = 1, \ldots, M) \tag{37}$$

- **Step 4**: Following (5), $N(\overline{\boldsymbol{Bv}}^k)_j$ can be reconstructed by any $t+1$ participants and by further dividing N, $(\overline{\boldsymbol{Bv}}^k)_j$ is derived.

In such a manner, $\overline{\boldsymbol{Bv}}^k$ can be privately computed when $N \geq 3$. When $N = 2$, given the reconstructed result and his own intermediate state, one participant can derive the intermediate state of the other. This is inevitable here but we can adopt the method in [10] to alleviate this problem. The basic idea is to add controllable noise to the intermediate states to satisfy the requirements of differential privacy. Consequently, given $\overline{\boldsymbol{Bv}}^k$, the iterations of (32)–(34) can be locally computed without revealing $\boldsymbol{B}_i \boldsymbol{v}_i$ to others.

6   Performance Evaluation

The performance of the proposed FSVM protocol is twofold, efficiency and effectiveness. Before demonstrating experimental results, we first offer the settings of the experiments. The following experiments are carried on a desktop running the 64-bit Ubuntu-18.04.1 operating system with Intel Core i7 CPU and 64 GB memory. Different participants are simulated by different threads in this desktop. To achieve the CMP function, the open-source ABY framework proposed by [14] is adopted. Specifically, we set the bit length $l = 32$ and thus all the arithmetic shares are in the range of $(0, 2^l)$. The secret sharing scheme is implemented by C++ and multiplication triples are generated following [18]. By these settings, the time efficiency is evaluated. As for the effectiveness, the FSVM is implemented on the MNIST, which is a widely utilized dataset of handwritten digits in the area of artificial intelligence[1].

---

[1] http://yann.lecun.com/exdb/mnist/.

6.1 Efficiency Evaluation

Since secret sharing is introduced to achieve privacy preserving goals, there is a great concern on the time efficiency when combining secret sharing with ADMM iterations. In the experiments, the communications among the participants are realized via sockets and information exchanging is in a pair-wise manner (referred as the client and server in sockets). Thus, the running time for any two participants privately exchanging intermediates in one iteration is evaluated and the final result is derived as the average of the outputs for running each experiment 100 times.

Here, the number of operations and the amount of data to be exchanged are determined by the number of features D. Table 1 presents experimental results when D varies from 100 to 1000 with a step size of 100. As there is a pre-computing phase to generate $\{q_{i,i+1}^k\}$ and $\{q_{i+1,i}^k\}$ for protecting intermediate states, the implementation of FSVM-C is divided by an offline phase for this pre-computation and an online phase for secretly exchanging intermediate states. In addition, the running time for the method in [11] is evaluated for comparison with FSVM-C when data partitioning by examples. Table 1 presents the experimental results related to time efficiency.

Table 1. Efficiency evaluation for FSVM (s)

D	FSVM-C			Method in [11]	FSVM-S
	Q	Offline	Online		
100	100	0.214	$2.76E-4$	0.0698	$2.19E-4$
200	200	0.810	$3.10E-4$	0.155	$2.75E-4$
300	300	1.83	$3.33E-4$	0.217	$2.92E-4$
400	400	3.24	$3.70E-4$	0.297	$3.07E-4$
500	500	5.13	$4.01E-4$	0.362	$3.20E-4$
600	600	7.46	$4.16E-4$	0.432	$3.32E-4$
700	700	10.02	$4.53E-4$	0.509	$3.44E-4$
800	800	13.21	$4.82E-4$	0.615	$3.67E-4$
900	900	16.60	$5.08E-4$	0.647	$3.79E-4$
1000	1000	20.56	$5.35E-4$	0.722	$3.98E-4$

Apparently, when D increases, more data are needed to be computed and transmitted and there is no doubt that the running time increases for the method in [11], FSVM-C and FSVM-S. Focusing on the running time of the offline phase in FSVM-C, the goal is to generate enough random numbers that satisfy the conditions of (14) and (15) and each is utilized in one iteration. Thus the running time for this phase is independent of D determined by the number of random numbers to be generated (referred as Q). When Q linearly increases from 100 to

1000 with a step size of 100, the running time approximately increases quadratically. This is because when the operation CMP is introduced in this phase, it needs Q additions and $Q(Q-1)/2$ comparisons via secret sharing. Note that additions are very fast and the running time is dominated by the number of comparisons. With respect to the running time for the online phase in FSVM-C, the method in [11] and FSVM-S, it linearly increases when D increases. Specifically, in the case of data partitioning by examples, benefiting from the offline phase, the running time for FSVM-C is about 1350 times lower than that for the method [11]. This significant improvement is due to the heavy computation overhead introduced by additional homomorphic encryption in [11]. As for FSVM-S, data are partitioned by features and the number of features to be considered by the enrolled participants is smaller than that of FSVM-C. It is direct that the running time for FSVM-S is smaller than of that for FSVM-C.

6.2 Effectiveness Evaluation

To evaluated the effectiveness of the proposed FSVM scheme, we implement it on the popular MNIST dataset. For binary classifications, the images of digit 2 and digit 9 are chosen with positive and negative labels. As each image is of size 28 by 28 pixels, each data entry consists of 784 features. After filtering, there are 5470 and 5454 images of digit 2 and 9, respectively. Thus, for the case of data partitioning by examples, there are 10924 data entries that are randomly distributed to N participants. For the case of data partitioning by features, M is set to 5000 and N participants evenly share these features. Here, we set $N = 2, 3, 4,$ and 5. For the test set, the numbers of images of 2 and 9 are both 500. Due to space limitation, the prediction accuracy, denoted by P_a, is utilized here as the performance matrix for effectiveness evaluation.

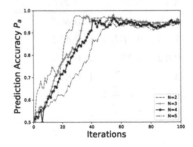

Fig. 2. Prediction Accuracy P_a versus iterations, where the FSVM-C is implemented and N = 2, 3, 4, and 5.

As is shown in Fig. 2, the prediction accuracy of FSVM-C is offered as the number of iterations increases. At the beginning, the initial states are randomly selected and the prediction here is like a random guess. Thus, all the curves starts from around 0.5. It is explicit that all the P_as converges to around 0.95

when the values of N vary but the speeds for convergence are different. In the case where $N = 2$, P_a converges with the highest speed and the convergence speed for $N = 5$ is the lowest. This is because as N increases larger, the number of data entries hold by each participant becomes smaller and less data entries means that the participant mainly relies on the received intermediate states from others to derive a more generalized classifier. For the worst case where $N = 5$, P_a converges after around 50 iterations and this implies that the number of random values to be generated for privacy preserving by each participant, namely Q, can be set slightly larger than 50.

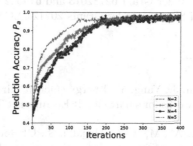

Fig. 3. Prediction Accuracy P_a versus iterations, where the FSVM-S is implemented and N = 2, 3, 4, and 5.

Figure 3 depicts the prediction accuracy P_a of FSVM-S versus the number of iterations where N varies from 2 to 5. The experimental results here are similar to those of FSVM-C. All the curves starts from near 0.5 due to the random selection of initial states and larger N means slower convergence speed. Unlike FSVM-C where each participant can obtain partial information of the global data distribution from the locally held data, any independent participant in FSVM-S can only have some of the features to be considered for classification and the relationships among these features might not be obvious. As a result, less information about the global data distribution would be derived when FSVM-S is implemented where data are partitioned by features. Hence, P_a of FSVM-S has a slower convergence speed here than that of FSVM-C and even for the best case when $N = 2$, P_a converges after more than 100 iterations.

7   Conclusion

In this paper, we propose the FSVM scheme to construct SVM classifiers in a distributed and privacy-preserving manner. Since there are two cases where data are partitioned by examples and features, the FSVM consists of FSVM-C and FSVM-S to deal with these two cases, respectively. In FSVM-C, the new ADMM in [11] that allows time-varying matrices is incorporated with secret sharing to achieve the privacy-preserving goal in a more efficient manner. Also, there is no need for a trusted third-party to generate keys. With respect to FSVM-S, we derive the closed form of the ADMM iterations and the Shamir secret sharing is introduced to protect intermediate states. By implementing the FSVM scheme on the dataset MNIST, the efficiency and effectiveness of both FSVM-S and FSVM-C are verified by comprehensive experimental results. Moreover, these experimental results also present an explicit guideline for implementing the proposed FSVM scheme in practical smart city applications.

Acknowledgement. This work is supported by the National Key Research and Development Program of China under Grant 2021YFB2700600, the National Natural Science Foundation of China under Grant 62132013 and 61902292, the Key Research and Development Programs of Shaanxi under Grants 2021ZDLGY06-03.

References

1. Dong, Y., Guo, S., Liu, J., Yang, Y.: Energy-efficient fair cooperation fog computing in mobile edge networks for smart city. IEEE Internet Things J. **6**(5), 7543–7554 (2019)
2. Sadiq, A.S., Faris, H., Ala'M, A.-Z., Mirjalili, S., Ghafoor, K.Z.: Fraud detection model based on multi-verse features extraction approach for smart city applications. In: Smart Cities Cybersecurity and Privacy, pp. 241–251. Elsevier (2019)
3. Rasheed, W., Tang, T.B.: Anomaly detection of moderate traumatic brain injury using auto-regularized multi-instance one-class SVM. IEEE Trans. Neural Syst. Rehabil. Eng. **28**, 83–93 (2019)
4. Hu, J., Ma, D., Liu, C., Shi, Z., Yan, H., Hu, C.: Network security situation prediction based on MR-SVM. IEEE Access **7**, 130 937–130 945 (2019)
5. Naranjo, P.G.V., Pooranian, Z., Shojafar, M., Conti, M., Buyya, R.: FOCAN: a fog-supported smart city network architecture for management of applications in the internet of everything environments. J. Parallel Distrib. Comput. **132**, 274–283 (2019)
6. Qu, Y., Yu, S., Zhou, W., Peng, S., Wang, G., Xiao, K.: Privacy of things: emerging challenges and opportunities in wireless internet of things. IEEE Wirel. Commun. **25**(6), 91–97 (2018)
7. Qu, Y., et al.: Decentralized privacy using blockchain-enabled federated learning in fog computing. IEEE Internet of Things J. **7**, 5171–5183 (2020)
8. Forero, P.A., Cano, A., Giannakis, G.B.: Consensus-based distributed support vector machines. J. Mach. Learn. Res. **11**(May), 1663–1707 (2010)
9. Boyd, S., Parikh, N., Chu, E., Peleato, B., Eckstein, J., et al.: Distributed optimization and statistical learning via the alternating direction method of multipliers. Found. Trends® Mach. Learn. **3**(1), 1–122 (2011)
10. Zhang, T., Zhu, Q.: Dynamic differential privacy for ADMM-based distributed classification learning. IEEE Trans. Inf. Forensics Secur. **12**(1), 172–187 (2016)
11. Zhang, C., Ahmad, M., Wang, Y.: ADMM based privacy-preserving decentralized optimization. IEEE Trans. Inf. Forensics Secur. **14**(3), 565–580 (2018)
12. Kairouz, P., et al.: Advances and open problems in federated learning. arXiv preprint arXiv:1912.04977 (2019)
13. Mozaffari, H., Houmansadr, A.: Heterogeneous private information retrieval. In: NDSS (2020)

14. Demmler, D., Schneider, T., Zohner, M.: ABY - a framework for efficient mixed-protocol secure two-party computation. In: NDSS (2015)
15. Shamir, A.: How to share a secret. Commun. ACM **22**(11), 612–613 (1979)
16. Kolesnikov, V., Sadeghi, A.-R., Schneider, T.: Improved garbled circuit building blocks and applications to auctions and computing minima. In: Garay, J.A., Miyaji, A., Otsuka, A. (eds.) CANS 2009. LNCS, vol. 5888, pp. 1–20. Springer, Heidelberg (2009). https://doi.org/10.1007/978-3-642-10433-6_1
17. Beaver, D.: Efficient multiparty protocols using circuit randomization. In: Feigenbaum, J. (ed.) CRYPTO 1991. LNCS, vol. 576, pp. 420–432. Springer, Heidelberg (1992). https://doi.org/10.1007/3-540-46766-1_34
18. Asharov, G., Lindell, Y., Schneider, T., Zohner, M.: More efficient oblivious transfer and extensions for faster secure computation. In: Proceedings of the 2013 ACM SIGSAC Conference on Computer & Communications Security, pp. 535–548 (2013)

Author Index

© ICST Institute for Computer Sciences, Social Informatics and Telecommunications Engineering 2023
Published by Springer Nature Switzerland AG 2023. All Rights Reserved
S. Yu et al. (Eds.): TridentCom 2022, LNICST 489, p. 169, 2023.
https://doi.org/10.1007/978-3-031-33458-0

Printed in the United States
by Baker & Taylor Publisher Services

Printed in the United States
by Baker & Taylor Publisher Services